THE FICTION TUTOR

DAVID MADDEN

Louisiana State University

Holt, Rinehart and Winston, Inc.

Fort Worth   Chicago   San Francisco

Philadelphia   Montreal   Toronto   London

Sydney   Tokyo

ISBN: 0-03-014289-X

Address for editorial correspondence: Holt, Rinehart and Winston, Inc., 301 Commerce Street, Suite 3700, Fort Worth, TX 76102

Address for orders: Holt, Rinehart and Winston, Inc., 6277 Sea Harbor Drive, Orlando, Florida 32887. 1-800-782-4479, or 1-800-433-0001 (in Florida)

PRINTED IN THE UNITED STATES OF AMERICA

0 1 2 3   066 9 8 7 6 5 4 32 1

Holt, Rinehart and Winston, Inc.
The Dryden Press
Saunders College Publishing

CONTENTS

Preface

PREFACE

The purpose of this handbook is to provide a brief introduction to the art of reading, the elements and the techniques of fiction, and the art of writing about fiction.

As a student of fiction, consider setting this as your purpose: to understand why and how the writer affects your emotions, your imagination, and your intellect.

I am myself a writer of short stories and novels and I will trace the process from the writer's inspiration to write a story to the student's paper about a story, to show a continuity in that process and to show parallels between the writing process and the reading process.

This book is designed to help students develop an ability to respond as fully as possible—emotionally, imaginatively, and intellectually—to the art and substance of fiction.

To serve that intention, I have selected three stories for illustration, each using a different point of view and style: Flannery O'Connor's "A Good Man Is Hard to Find" (omniscient), Ralph Ellison's "Battle Royal" (first person), and Katherine Mansfield's "Miss Brill" (central intelligence).

The critical sections present as clearly and simply as possible the fundamental critical principles that will give you a means of understanding, evaluating, and appreciating many different kinds of stories.

Elements in your everyday life parallel the nature, techniques, and effects of fiction. When I can do it, I will show, with examples from the three stories, a coherent relationship among the act of writing fiction, the act of reading fiction, and the act of discussing and writing about fiction. What you do in every-day life often parallels what the writer has done in the creative process; in reading and in writing, your activities are similar to the fiction writer's.

"The Art of Reading Fiction" takes up several aspects of the reading experience. The three stories are offered first with little comment. Then emotional, imaginative, and intellectual responses are described, with illustrations taken from the three stories.

Recognizing that most students choose to read commercial fiction, I briefly discuss some of the different ways writers of commercial and literary fiction handle the elements and tech-niques of fiction.

To narrow the distance between writers and readers, I discuss the parallels between the act of writing fiction and the act of reading fiction. Writers may be as obtuse in the first draft as many students imagine themselves to be in the first reading of a story, or during class discussion. The writer writes and revises for the reader; the reader re-reads to make the fullest response.

Finally, I explain some differences between the usual way we all read and the way we read when we are studying the nature and effects of fiction.

I then provide discussion of "The Art of Writing Fiction."

Using one of the three stories to illustrate each, I describe the basic elements of fiction—character, setting, story and plot, conflict, and theme—and how they interact. Then I demonstrate how writers deliberately use various techniques in their handling of the elements of fiction to affect their readers.

Effective development of character, setting, story, conflict, and theme depends upon the writer's handling of point of view (as a technique, rather than as an attitude). The writer's control of the point-of-view technique he or she has chosen determines the effect of every other technique in the story. But this technique seems to give both writers and readers more trouble than any other aspect of fiction. Using the three stories as examples, I attempt to explain the workings of point of view as clearly as possible, again showing parallels in our everyday lives.

I show how the author's style in a story is determined not only by the sensibility and intellect of the narrator, but by the author's choice of point-of-view technique, with the three stories illustrating aspects of style.

In this section, I also draw on everyday life and the three stories to illustrate ways in which writers use such devices as context and implication, comparison and contrast, symbol, allusion, and irony to enhance the effects of character, setting, story, conflict, and theme, as controlled by point of view and style.

A brief section describes the various commercial and literary genres, including innovative fiction. Three review lists follow: "Considerations as You Read," "Considerations as You Discuss," and "Master Review Questions that Apply to Most Fiction."

A "Glossary of Critical Terms" appears at the back of the book.

In Chapter Three, "The Art of Writing About Fiction," using Flannery O'Connor's "A Good Man Is Hard to Find" and a student essay at various stages for illustration, I guide you through the writing of different kinds of essays about fiction, description, interpretation, analysis, comparison and contrast, personal evaluation, through the stages of writing: prewriting activities, the rough draft, the serious first draft, what to look for in the revision process. I include, as outside reading, essays by O'Connor and Caroline Gordon on O'Connor's story.

I conclude with a "Master List of Writing Topics That Apply to Most Fiction."

Some of the critical material in this book is an adaptation of passages from my earlier text, *Studies in the Short Story* (edited with Virgil Scott) and my book *Revising Fiction* (with permission of New American Library).

On this book, as on many others, Peggy Bach has given me invaluable advice.

Virgil Scott and I edited several editions of *Studies in the Short Story*; I want to acknowledge here, with gratitude, that his analysis of the workings of context and implication made me see much more clearly the crucial function of that technique.

I wish to thank the following reviewers:

Dorothy Bankston, Louisiana State University
Walter Anderson, University of California, Los Angeles
Roger Applebee, University of Illinois—Urbana
Victoria Arana-Robinson, Howard University
Olga Asal, Florida State University
Carol Barnes, Kansas State University
Ernest Bufkin, University of Geogria
Peter Carino, Indiana State University
Phillip Castille, University of Houston
Sumita Chaudhery, Schoolcraft College
Tom Collins, University of Arizona
James Cowan, University of North Carolina at Chapel Hill
Raymond Gozzi, University of Massachusetts at Amherst
Richard Harmetz, Los Angeles Trade Technical College
Barbara Haxby, Triton College
William Holtz, University of Missouri—Columbia
Don Kunz, University of Rhode Island
Rosemary Lanshe, Broward Community College
Lee Leeson, Pepperdine University
Susan Lohafer, University of Iowa
Helen Marlboro, DePaul University
Edward Martin, Middlebury College
Noralyn Masselink, Hofstra University
C. L. Proudfit, University of Colorado—Boulder
Margaret Rowe, Purdue University
Betty Townsend, University of Maryland

I very much appreciate Charlyce Jones Owen's editorial guidance. Diane D. LeNoir and Joyce M. Grant, Louisiana State University Text Processing, typeset the manuscript.

Baton Rouge　　　　　　　　　*David Madden*
November 1989　　　　　　　*Louisiana State University*

In Memory of
Boyd Litzinger,
Master Teacher

ONE
THE ART OF READING FICTION

The following three stories are offered without comment, so you may, as much as possible, read them in the way you usually read fiction. Normally, you would, of course, stop reading if the story did not quickly "hook" your interest. If you feel a desire to stop, you might mark that point, then later ask yourself how the story failed to "grab" your interest. Give free rein to your taste, your normal, natural responses and reactions, sympathetic or not.

Once you have read all three stories at your normal speed, go one step further than you usually do when reading fiction in magazines; reread each story, trying to become aware of the methods the authors used to achieve their effects on you. Looking back, ask, "*How* did the writer *do* that to me?" Mark passages and make marginal notes based on your present knowledge of the nature, techniques, and effects of fiction. (Markings do not affect the buy-back value of texts.)

This handbook will provide you with a vocabulary and concepts for analyzing what *happens* in fiction and *how*; you will contemplate the elements of fiction with critical deliberateness. But for these first three stories, simply focus sharply on your own responses to the techniques the writer employs. Each of these stories will provide illustrations for the points made later about the elements of fiction, and the art of writing fiction and about the art of reading and writing about fiction.

1

A GOOD MAN IS HARD TO FIND
by Flannery O'Connor

The Grandmother didn't want to go to Florida. She wanted to visit some of her connections in east Tennessee and she was seizing at every chance to change Bailey's mind. Bailey was the son she lived with, her only boy. He was sitting on the edge of his chair at the table, bent over the orange sports section of the journal. "Now look here, Bailey," she said, "see here, read this," and she stood with one hand on her thin hip and the other rattling the newspaper at his bald head. "Here this fellow that calls himself The Misfit is aloose from the Federal Pen and headed toward Florida and you read here what it says he did to these people. Just you read it. I wouldn't take my children in any direction with a criminal like that aloose in it. I couldn't answer to my conscience if I did."

Bailey didn't look up from his reading so she wheeled around then and faced the children's mother, a young woman in slacks, whose face was as broad and innocent as a cabbage and was tied around with a green head-kerchief that had two points on the top like a rabbit's ears. She was sitting on the sofa, feeding the baby his apricots out of a jar. "The children have been to Florida before," the old lady said. "You all ought to take them somewhere else for a change so they would see different parts of the world and be broad. They never have been to east Tennessee."

The children's mother didn't seem to hear her but the eight-year-old boy, John Wesley, a stocky child with glasses, said, "If you don't want to go to Florida, why dontcha stay at home?" He and the little girl, June Star, were reading the funny papers on the floor.

"She wouldn't stay at home to be queen for a day," June Star said without raising her yellow head.

"Yes and what would you do if this fellow, The Misfit, caught you?" the grandmother asked.

"I'd smack his face," John Wesley said.

"She wouldn't stay at home for a million bucks," June Star said. "Afraid she'd miss something. She has to go everywhere we go."

"All right, Miss," the grandmother said. "Just remember that the next time you want me to curl your hair."

June Star said her hair was naturally curly.

The next morning the grandmother was the first one in the car, ready to go. She had her big black valise that looked like the head of a hippopotamus in one corner, and underneath it she was hiding a basket with Pitty Sing, the cat, in it. She didn't intend for the cat to be left alone in the house for three days because he would miss her too much and she was afraid he might brush against one of the gas burners and accidentally asphyxiate himself. Her son, Bailey, didn't like to arrive at a motel with a cat.

She sat in the middle of the back seat with John Wesley and June Star on either side of her. Bailey and the children's mother and the baby sat in front and they left Atlanta at eight forty-five with the mileage on the car at 55890. The grandmother wrote this down because she thought it would be interesting to say how many miles they had been when they got back. It took them twenty minutes to reach the outskirts of the city.

The old lady settled herself comfortably, removing her white cotton gloves and putting them up with her purse on the shelf in front of the back window. The children's mother still had on slacks and still had her head tied up in a green kerchief, but the grandmother had on a navy blue straw sailor hat with a bunch of white violets on the brim and a navy blue dress with a small white dot in the print. Her collars and cuffs were white organdy trimmed with lace and at her neckline she had pinned a purple spray of cloth violets containing a sachet. In case of an accident, anyone seeing her dead on the highway would know at once that she was a lady.

She said she thought it was going to be a good day for driving, neither too hot nor too cold, and she cautioned Bailey that the speed limit was fifty-five miles an hour and that the patrolmen hid themselves behind billboards and small clumps of trees and sped out after you before you had a chance to slow down. She pointed out interesting details of the scenery: Stone Mountain; the blue granite that in some places came up to both sides of the highway; the brilliant red clay banks slightly streaked with purple; and the various crops that made rows of green lace-work on the ground.

The trees were full of silver-white sunlight and the meanest of them sparkled. The children were reading comic magazines and their mother had gone back to sleep.

"Let's go through Georgia fast so we won't have to look at it much," John Wesley said.

"If I were a little boy," said the grandmother, "I wouldn't talk about my native state that way. Tennessee has the mountains and Georgia has the hills."

"Tennessee is just a hillbilly dumping ground," John Wesley said, "and Georgia is a lousy state too."

"You said it," June Star said.

"In my time," said the grandmother, folding her thin veined fingers, "children were more respectful of their native states and their parents and everything else. People did right then. Oh look at the cute little pickaninny!" she said and pointed to a Negro child standing in the door of a shack. "Wouldn't that make a picture, now?" she asked and they all turned and looked at the little Negro out of the back window. He waved.

"He didn't have any britches on," June Star said.

"He probably didn't have any," the grandmother explained. "Little niggers in the country don't have things like we do. If I could paint, I'd paint that picture," she said.

The children exchanged comic books.

The grandmother offered to hold the baby and the children's mother passed him over the front seat to her. She set him on her knee and bounced him and told him about the things they were passing. She rolled her eyes and screwed up her mouth and stuck her leathery thin face into his smooth bland one. Occasionally he gave her a faraway smile. They passed a large cotton field with five or six graves fenced in the middle of it, like a small island.

"Look at the graveyard!" the grandmother said, pointing it out. "That was the old family burying ground. That belonged to the plantation."

"Where's the plantation?" John Wesley asked.

"Gone With the Wind," said the grandmother. "Ha. Ha."

When the children finished all the comic books they had brought, they opened the lunch and ate it. The grandmother ate a peanut butter sandwich and an olive and would not let the children throw the box and the paper napkins out the window. When there was nothing else to do they played a game by choosing a cloud and making the other two guess what shape it suggested. John Wesley took one the shape of a cow and June Star guessed a cow and John Wesley said, no, an automobile, and June Star said he didn't play fair, and they began to slap each other over the grandmother.

The grandmother said she would tell them a story if they would keep quiet. When she told a story, she rolled her eyes and waved her head and was very dramatic. She said once when she was a maiden lady she had been courted by a Mr. Edgar Atkins Teagarden from Jasper, Georgia. She said he was a very good-looking man and a gentleman and that he brought her a watermelon every Saturday afternoon with his initials cut in it, E. A. T. Well, one Saturday, she said, Mr. Teagarden brought the watermelon and there was nobody at home and he left it on the front porch and returned in his buggy to Jasper, but she never got the watermelon, she said, because a nigger boy ate it when he saw the initials, E. A. T.! This story tickled John Wesley's funny bone and he giggled and giggled but June Star didn't think it was any good. She said she wouldn't marry a man that just brought her a watermelon on Saturday. The grandmother said she would have done well to marry Mr. Teagarden because he was a gentleman and had bought Coca-Cola stock when it first came out and that he had died only a few years ago, a very wealthy man.

They stopped at The Tower for barbecued sandwiches. The Tower was a part stucco and part wood filling station and dance hall set in a clearing outside of Timothy. A fat man named Red Sammy Butts ran it and there were signs stuck here and there on the building and for miles up and down the highway saying, TRY RED SAMMY'S FAMOUS BARBECUE. NONE LIKE FAMOUS RED SAMMY'S! RED SAM! THE FAT BOY WITH THE HAPPY LAUGH! A VETERAN! RED SAMMY'S YOUR MAN!

Red Sammy was lying on the bare ground outside The Tower with his head under a truck while a gray monkey about a foot high, chained to a small chinaberry tree, chattered nearby. The monkey sprang back into the tree and got on the highest limb as soon as he saw the children jump out of the car and run toward him.

Inside, The Tower was a long dark room with a counter at one end and tables at the other and dancing space in the middle. They all sat down at a board table next to the nickelodeon and Red Sam's wife, a tall burnt-brown woman with hair and eyes lighter than her skin, came and took their order. The children's mother put a dime in the machine and played "The Tennessee Waltz," and the grandmother said that tune always made her want to dance. She asked Bailey if he would like to dance but he only glared at her. He didn't have a naturally sunny disposition like she did and trips made him nervous. The grandmother's brown eyes were very bright. She swayed her head from side to side and pretended she was dancing in her chair. June Star said play something she could tap to so the children's mother put in another dime and played a fast number and June Star stepped out onto the dance floor and did her tap routine.

"Ain't she cute?" Red Sam's wife said, leaning over the counter. "Would you like to come be my little girl?"

"No I certainly wouldn't," June Star said. "I wouldn't live in a broken-down place like this for a million bucks!" and she ran back to the table.

"Ain't she cute?" the woman repeated, stretching her mouth politely.

"Aren't you ashamed?" hissed the grandmother.

Red Sam came in and told his wife to quit lounging on the counter and hurry up with these people's order. His khaki trousers reached just to his hip bones and his stomach hung over them like a sack of meal swaying under his shirt. He came over and sat down at a table nearby and let out a combination sigh and yodel.

"You can't win," he said. "You can't win," and he wiped his sweating red face off with a gray handkerchief. "These days you don't know who to trust," he said. "Ain't that the truth?"

"People are certainly not nice like they used to be," said the grandmother.

"Two fellers come in here last week," Red Sammy said, "driving a Chrysler. It was a old beat-up car but it was a good one and these boys looked all right to me. Said they worked at the mill and you know I let them fellers charge the gas they bought? Now why did I do that?"

"Because you're a good man!" the grandmother said at once.

"Yes'm, I suppose so," Red Sam said as if he were struck with this answer.

His wife brought the orders, carrying the five plates all at once without a tray, two in each hand and one balanced on her arm.

"It isn't a soul in this green world of God's that you can trust," she said. "And I don't count nobody out of that, not nobody," she repeated, looking at Red Sammy.

"Did you read about that criminal, The Misfit, that's escaped?" asked the grandmother.

"I wouldn't be a bit surprised if he didn't attact this place right here," said the woman. "If he hears about it being here, I wouldn't be none surprised to see him. If he hears it's two cent in the cash register, I wouldn't be a tall surprised if he . . . "

"That'll do," Red Sam said. "Go bring these people their Co'-Colas," and the woman went off to get the rest of the order.

"A good man is hard to find," Red Sammy said. "Everything is getting terrible. I remember the day you could go off and leave your screen door unlatched. Not no more."

He and the grandmother discussed better times. The old lady said that in her opinion Europe was entirely to blame for the way things were now. She said the way Europe acted you would think we were made of money and Red Sam said it was no use talking about it, she was exactly right. The children ran outside into the white sunlight and looked at the monkey in the lacy chinaberry tree. He was busy catching fleas on himself and biting each one carefully between his teeth as if it were a delicacy.

They drove off again into the hot afternoon. The grandmother took cat naps and woke up every few minutes with her own snoring. Outside of Toombsboro she woke up and recalled an old plantation that she had visited in this neighborhood once when she was a young lady. She said the house had six white columns across the front and that there was an avenue of oaks leading up to it and two little wooden trellis arbors on either side in front where you sat down with your suitor after a stroll in the garden. She recalled exactly which road to turn off to get to it. She knew that Bailey would not be willing to lose any time looking at an old house, but the more she talked about it, the more she wanted to see it once again and find out if the little twin arbors were still standing. "There was a secret panel in this house," she said craftily, not telling the truth but wishing that she were, "and the story went that all the family silver was hidden in it when Sherman came through but it was never found . . . "

"Hey!" John Wesley said. "Let's go see it! We'll find it! We'll poke all the woodwork and find it! Who lives there? Where do you turn off at? Hey Pop, can't we turn off there?"

"We never have seen a house with a secret panel!" June Star shrieked. "Let's go to the house with the secret panel! Hey Pop, can't we go see the house with the secret panel!"

"It's not far from here, I know," the grandmother said. "It wouldn't take over twenty minutes ... "

Bailey was looking straight ahead. His jaw was as rigid as a horseshoe. "No," he said.

The children began to yell and scream that they wanted to see the house with the secret panel. John Wesley kicked the back of the front seat and June Star hung over her mother's shoulder and whined desperately into her ear that they never had any fun even on their vacation, that they could never do what THEY wanted to do. The baby began to scream and John Wesley kicked the back of the seat so hard that his father could feel the blows in his kidney. "All right!" he shouted and drew the car to a stop at the side of the road. "Will you all shut up? Will you all just shut up for one second? If you don't shut up, we won't go anywhere."

"It would be very educational for them," the grandmother murmured.

"All right," Bailey said, "but get this: this is the only time we're going to stop for anything like this. This is the one and only time."

"The dirt road that you have to turn down is about a mile back," the grandmother directed. "I marked it when we passed."

"A dirt road," Bailey groaned.

After they had turned around and were headed toward the dirt road, the grandmother recalled other points about the house, the beautiful glass over the front doorway and the candle-lamp in the hall. John Wesley said that the secret panel was probably in the fireplace.

"You can't go inside this house," Bailey said. "You don't know who lives there."

"While you all talk to the people in front, I'll run around behind and get in a window," John Wesley suggested.

"We'll all stay in the car," his mother said.

They turned onto the dirt road and the car raced roughly along in a swirl of pink dust. The grandmother recalled the times when there were no paved roads and thirty miles was a day's journey. The dirt road was hilly and there were sudden washes in it and sharp curves on dangerous embankments. All at once they would be on a hill, looking down over the blue tops of trees for miles around, then the next minute, they would be in a red depression with the dust-coated trees looking down on them.

"This place had better turn up in a minute," Bailey said, "or I'm going to turn around."

The road looked as if no one had traveled on it in months.

"It's not much farther," the grandmother said and just as she said it, a horrible thought came to her. The thought was so embarrassing that she turned red in the face and her eyes dilated and her feet jumped up, upsetting her valise in the corner. The instant the valise moved, the newspaper top she had over the basket under it rose with a snarl and Pitty Sing, the cat, sprang onto Bailey's shoulder. The children were thrown to the floor and their mother, clutching the baby, was thrown out the door onto the ground; the old lady was thrown into the front seat. The car turned over once and landed right-side-up in a gulch off the side of the road. Bailey remained in the driver's seat with the cat—gray-striped with a broad white face and an orange nose—clinging to his neck like a caterpillar.

As soon as the children saw they could move their arms and legs, they scrambled out of the car, shouting, "We've had an ACCIDENT!" The grandmother was curled up under the dashboard, hoping she was injured so that Bailey's wrath would not come down on her all at once. The horrible thought she had had before the accident was that the house she had remembered so vividly was not in Georgia but in Tennessee.

Bailey removed the cat from his neck with both hands and flung it out the window against the side of a pine tree. Then he got out of the car and started looking for the children's mother. She was sitting against the side of the red gutted ditch, holding the screaming baby, but she only had a cut down her face and a broken shoulder. "We've had an ACCIDENT!" the children screamed in a frenzy of delight.

"But nobody's killed," June Star said with disappointment as the grandmother limped out of the car, her hat still pinned to her head but the broken front brim standing up at a jaunty angle and the violet spray hanging off the side. They all sat down in the ditch, except the children, to recover from the shock. They were all shaking.

"Maybe a car will come along," said the children's mother hoarsely.

"I believe I have injured an organ," said the grandmother, pressing her side, but no one answered her. Bailey's teeth were clattering.

He had on a yellow sport shirt with bright blue parrots designed in it and his face was as yellow as the shirt. The grandmother decided that she would not mention that the house was in Tennessee.

The road was about ten feet above and they could see only the tops of the trees on the other side of it. Behind the ditch they were sitting in there were more woods, tall and dark and deep. In a few minutes they saw a car some distance away on top of a hill, coming slowly as if the occupants were watching them. The grandmother stood up and waved both arms dramatically to attract their attention. The car continued to come on slowly, disappeared around a bend and appeared again, moving even slower, on top of the hill they had gone over. It was a big black battered hearselike automobile. There were three men in it.

It came to a stop just over them and for some minutes, the driver looked down with a steady expressionless gaze to where they were sitting, and didn't speak.   Then he turned his head and muttered something to the other two and they got out.   One was a fat boy in black trousers and a red sweat shirt with a silver stallion embossed on the front of it. He moved around on the right side of them and stood staring, his mouth partly open in a kind of loose grin. The other had on khaki pants and a blue striped coat and a gray hat pulled down very low, hiding most of his face. He came around slowly on the left side. Neither spoke.

The driver got out of the car and stood by the side of it, looking down at them. He was an older man than the other two. His hair was just beginning to gray and he wore silver-rimmed spectacles that gave him a scholarly look. He had a long creased face and didn't have on any shirt or undershirt. He had on blue jeans that were too tight for him and was holding a black hat and a gun.

The two boys also had guns.

"We've had an ACCIDENT!" the children screamed.

The grandmother had the peculiar feeling that the bespectacled man was someone she knew. His face was as familiar to her as if she had known him all her life but she could not recall who he was.

He moved away from the car and began to come down the embankment, placing his feet carefully so that he wouldn't slip. He had on tan and white shoes and no socks, and his ankles were red and thin. "Good afternoon," he said. "I see you all had you a little spill."

"We turned over twice!" said the grandmother.

"Oncet," he corrected. "We seen it happen. Try their car and see will it run, Hiram," he said quietly to the boy with the gray hat..

"What you got that gun for?" John Wesley asked. "Whatcha gonna do with that gun?"

"Lady," the man said to the children's mother, "would you mind calling them children to sit down by you? Children make me nervous. I want all you all to sit down right together there where you're at."

"What are you telling US what to do for?" June Star asked.

Behind them the line of woods gaped like a dark open mouth.

"Come here," said their mother.

"Look here now," Bailey began suddenly, "we're in a predicament! We're in ... "

The grandmother shrieked. She scrambled to her feet and stood staring. "You're The Misfit!" she said. "I recognized you at once!"

"Yes'm," the man said, smiling slightly as if he were pleased in spite of himself to be known, "but it would have been better for all of you, lady, if you hadn't of reckernized me."

Bailey turned his head sharply and said something to his mother that shocked even the children. The old lady began to cry and The Misfit reddened.

"Lady," he said, "don't you get upset. Sometimes a man says things he don't mean. I don't reckon he meant to talk to you thataway."

"You wouldn't shoot a lady, would you?" the grandmother said and removed a clean handkerchief from her cuff and began to slap at her eyes with it.

The Misfit pointed the toe of his shoe into the ground and made a little hole and then covered it up again. "I would hate to have to," he said.

"Listen," the grandmother almost screamed, "I know you're a good man. You don't look a bit like you have common blood. I know you must come from nice people!"

"Yes mam," he said, "finest people in the world." When he smiled he showed a row of strong white teeth. "God never made a finer woman than my mother and my daddy's heart was pure gold," he said. The boy with the red sweat shirt had come around behind them and was standing with his gun at his hip. The Misfit squatted down on the ground. "Watch them children, Bobby Lee," he said. "You know they make me nervous." He looked at the six of them huddled together in front of him and he seemed to be embarrassed as if he couldn't think of anything to say. "Ain't a cloud in the sky," he remarked, looking up at it. "Don't see no sun but don't see no cloud neither."

"Yes, it's a beautiful day," said the grandmother. "Listen," she said, "you shouldn't call yourself The Misfit because I know you're a good man at heart. I can just look at you and tell."

"Hush!" Bailey yelled. "Hush! Everybody shut up and let me handle this!" He was squatting in the position of a runner about to sprint forward but he didn't move.

"I pre-chate that, lady," The Misfit said and drew a little circle in the ground with the butt of his gun.

"It'll take a half a hour to fix this here car," Hiram called, looking over the raised hood of it.

"Well, first you and Bobby Lee get him and that little boy to step over yonder with you," The Misfit said, pointing to Bailey and John Wesley. "The boys want to ast you something," he said to Bailey. "Would you mind stepping back in them woods there with them ."

"Listen," Bailey began, "we're in a terrible predicament! Nobody realizes what this is," and his voice cracked. His eyes were as blue and intense as the parrots in his shirt and he remained perfectly still.

The grandmother reached up to adjust her hat brim as if she were going to the woods with him but it came off in her hand. She stood staring at it and after a second she let it fall on the ground. Hiram pulled Bailey up by the arm as if he were assisting an old man. John Wesley caught hold of his father's hand and Bobby Lee followed. They went off toward the woods and just as they reached the dark edge, Bailey turned and supporting himself against a gray naked pine trunk, he shouted, "I'll be back in a minute, Mamma, wait on me!"

"Come back this instant!" his mother shrilled but they all disappeared into the woods.

"Bailey Boy!" the grandmother called in a tragic voice but she found she was looking at The Misfit squatting on the ground in front of her. "I just know you're a good man," she said desperately. "You're not a bit common!"

"Nome, I ain't a good man," The Misfit said after a second as if he had considered her statement carefully, "but I ain't the worst in the world neither. My daddy said I was a different breed of dog from my brothers and sisters. 'You know,' Daddy said, 'it's some that can live their whole life out without asking about it and it's others has to know why it is, and this boy is one of the latters. He's going to be into everything!'" He put on his black hat and looked up suddenly and then away deep into the woods as if he were embarrassed again. "I'm sorry I don't have on a shirt before you ladies," he said, hunching his shoulders slightly. "We buried our clothes that we had on when we escaped and we're just making do until we can get better. We borrowed these from some folks we met," he explained.

"That's perfectly all right," the grandmother said. "Maybe Bailey has an extra shirt in his suitcase."

"I'll look and see terrectly," The Misfit said.

"Where are they taking him?" the children's mother screamed.

"Daddy was a card himself," The Misfit said. "You couldn't put anything over on him. He never got in trouble with the Authorities though. Just had the knack of handling them."

"You could be honest too if you'd only try," said the grandmother. "Think how wonderful it would be to settle down and live a comfortable life and not have to think about somebody chasing you all the time."

The Misfit kept scratching in the ground with the butt of his gun as if he were thinking about it. "Yes'm, somebody is always after you," he murmured.

The grandmother noticed how thin his shoulder blades were just behind his hat because she was standing up looking down on him.

"Do you ever pray?" she asked.

He shook his head. All she saw was the black hat wiggle between his shoulder blades. "Nome," he said.

There was a pistol shot from the woods, followed closely by another. Then silence. The old lady's head jerked around. She could hear the wind move through the tree tops like a long satisfied insuck of breath. "Bailey Boy!" she called.

"I was a gospel singer for a while," The Misfit said. "I been most everything. Been in the arm service, both land and sea, at home and abroad, been twict married, been an undertaker, been with the railroads, plowed Mother Earth, been in a tornado, seen a man burnt alive oncet," and looked up at the children's mother and the little girl who were sitting close together, their faces white and their eyes glassy; "I even seen a woman flogged," he said.

"Pray, pray, the grandmother began, pray, pray . . . "

"I never was a bad boy that I remember of," The Misfit said in an almost dreamy voice, "but somewheres along the line I done something wrong and got sent to the penitentiary. I was buried alive," and he looked up and held her attention to him by a steady stare.

"That's when you should have started to pray," she said. "What did you do to get sent to the penitentiary that first time?"

"Turn to the right, it was a wall," The Misfit said, looking up again at the cloudless sky. "Turn to the left, it was a wall. Look up it was a ceiling, look down it was a floor. I forget what I done, lady. I set there and set there, trying to remember what it was I done and I ain't recalled it to this day. Oncet in a while, I would think it was coming to me, but it never come."

"Maybe they put you in by mistake," the old lady said vaguely.

"Nome," he said. "It wasn't no mistake. They had the papers on me."

"You must have stolen something," she said.

The Misfit sneered slightly. "Nobody had nothing I wanted," he said. "It was a head-doctor at the penitentiary said what I had done was kill my daddy but I known that for a lie. My daddy died in nineteen ought nineteen of the epidemic flu and I never had a thing to do with it. He was buried in the Mount Hopewell Baptist churchyard and you can go there and see for yourself."

"If you would pray," the old lady said, "Jesus would help you."

"That's right," The Misfit said.

"Well then, why don't you pray?" she asked trembling with delight suddenly.

"I don't want no hep," he said. "I'm doing all right by myself."

Bobby Lee and Hiram came ambling back from the woods. Bobby Lee was dragging a yellow shirt with bright blue parrots in it.

"Thow me that shirt, Bobby Lee," The Misfit said. The shirt came flying at him and landed on his shoulder and he put it on. The grandmother couldn't name what the shirt reminded her of. "No, lady," The Misfit said while he was buttoning it up, "I found out the crime don't matter. You can do one thing or you can do another, kill a man or take a tire off his car, because sooner or later you're going to forget what it was you done and just be punished for it."

The children's mother had begun to make heaving noises as if she couldn't get her breath. "Lady," he asked, "would you and that little girl like to step off yonder with Bobby Lee and Hiram and join your husband?"

"Yes, thank you," the mother said faintly. Her left arm dangled helplessly and she was holding the baby, who had gone to sleep, in the other. "Hep that lady up, Hiram," The Misfit said as she struggled to climb out of the ditch, "and Bobby Lee, you hold onto that little girl's hand."

"I don't want to hold hands with him," June Star said. "He reminds me of a pig."

The fat boy blushed and laughed and caught her by the arm and pulled her off into the woods after Hiram and her mother.

Alone with The Misfit, the grandmother found that she had lost her voice. There was not a cloud in the sky nor any sun.

There was nothing around her but woods. She wanted to tell him that he must pray. She opened and closed her mouth several times before anything came out. Finally she found herself saying, "Jesus, Jesus," meaning, Jesus will help you, but the way she was saying it, it sounded as if she might be cursing.

"Yes'm," The Misfit said as if he agreed. "Jesus thown everything off balance. It was the same case with Him as with me except He hadn't committed any crime and they could prove I had committed one because they had the papers on me. Of course," he said, "they never shown me my papers. That's why I sign myself now. I said long ago, you get you a signature and sign everything you do and keep a copy of it. Then you'll know what you done and you can hold up the crime to the punishment and see do they match and in the end you'll have something to prove you ain't been treated right. I call myself The Misfit," he said, "because I can't make what all I done wrong fit what all I gone through in punishment."

There was a piercing scream from the woods, followed closely by a pistol report. "Does it seem right to you, lady, that one is punished a heap and another ain't punished at all?"

"Jesus!" the old lady cried. "You've got good blood! I know you wouldn't shoot a lady! I know you come from nice people! Pray! Jesus, you ought not to shoot a lady. I'll give you all the money I've got!"

"Lady," The Misfit said, looking beyond her far into the woods, "there never was a body that give the undertaker a tip."

There were two more pistol reports and the grandmother raised her head like a parched old turkey hen crying for water and called, "Bailey Boy, Bailey Boy!" as if her heart would break.

"Jesus was the only One that ever raised the dead," The Misfit continued, "and He shouldn't have done it. He thrown everything off balance. If He did what He said, then it's nothing for you to do but throw away everything and follow Him, and if He didn't, then it's nothing for you to do but enjoy the few minutes you got left the best way you can—by killing somebody or burning down his house or doing some other meanness to him. No pleasure but meanness," he said and his voice had become almost a snarl.

"Maybe He didn't raise the dead," the old lady mumbled, not knowing what she was saying and feeling so dizzy that she sank down in the ditch with her legs twisted under her.

"I wasn't there so I can't say He didn't," The Misfit said. "I wisht I had of been there," he said, hitting the ground with his fist. "It ain't right I wasn't there because if I had of been there I would of known. Listen lady," he said in a high voice, "if I had of been there I would of known and I wouldn't be like I am now." His voice seemed about to crack and the grandmother's head cleared for an instant. She saw the man's face twisted close to her own as if he were going to cry and she murmured, "Why you're one of my babies. You're one of my own children!" She reached out and touched him on the shoulder. The Misfit sprang back as if a snake had bitten him and shot her three times through the chest. Then he put his gun down on the ground and took off his glasses and began to clean them.

Hiram and Bobby Lee returned from the woods and stood over the ditch, looking down at the grandmother who half sat and half lay in a puddle of blood with her legs crossed under her like a child's and her face smiling up at the cloudless sky.

Without his glasses, The Misfit's eyes were red-rimmed and pale and defenseless-looking. "Take her off and throw her where you thrown the others," he said, picking up the cat that was rubbing itself against his leg.

"She was a talker, wasn't she?" Bobby Lee said, sliding down the ditch with a yodel.

"She would of been a good woman," The Misfit said, "if it had been somebody there to shoot her every minute of her life."

"Some fun!" Bobby Lee said.

"Shut up, Bobby Lee," The Misfit said. "It's no real pleasure in life."

2

BATTLE ROYAL
by Ralph Ellison

It goes a long way back, some twenty years. All my life I had been looking for something, and everywhere I turned someone tried to tell me what it was. I accepted their answers too, though they were often in contradiction and even self-contradictory. I was naive. I was looking for myself and asking everyone except myself questions which I, and only I, could answer. It took me a long time and much painful boomeranging of my expectations to achieve a realization everyone else appears to have been born with: That I am nobody but myself. But first I had to discover that I am an invisible man!

And yet I am no freak of nature, nor of history. I was in the cards, other things having been equal (or unequal) eighty-five years ago. I am not ashamed of my grandparents for having been slaves. I am only ashamed of myself for having at one time been ashamed. About eighty-five years ago they were told that they were free, united with others of our country in everything pertaining to the common good, and, in everything social, separate like the fingers of the hand. And they believed it. They exulted in it. They stayed in their place, worked hard, and brought up my father to do the same. But my grandfather is the one. He was an odd old guy, my grandfather, and I am told I take after him. It was he who caused the trouble. On his deathbed he called my father to him and said, "Son, after I'm gone I want you to keep up the good fight. I never told you, but our life is a war and I have been a traitor all my born days, a spy in the enemy's country ever since I give up my gun back in the Reconstruction. Live with your head in the lion's mouth. I want you to overcome 'em with yeses, undermine 'em with grins, agree 'em to death and destruction, let 'em swoller you till they vomit or bust wide open." They thought the old man had gone out of his mind. He had been the meekest of men. The younger children were rushed from the room, the shades drawn and the flame of the lamp turned so low that it sputtered on the wick like the old man's breathing. "Learn it to the younguns," he whispered fiercely; then he died.

But my folks were more alarmed over his last words than over his dying. It was as though he had not died at all, his words caused so much anxiety. I was warned emphatically to forget what he had said and indeed, this is the first time it has been mentioned outside the family circle. It had a tremendous effect upon me, however. I could never be sure of what he meant. Grandfather had been a quiet old man who never made any trouble, yet on his deathbed he had called himself a traitor and a spy, and he had spoken of his meekness as a dangerous activity. It became a constant puzzle which lay unanswered in the back of my mind. And whenever things went well for me I remembered my grandfather and felt guilty and uncomfortable. It was as though I was carrying out his advice in spite of myself. And to make it worse, everyone loved me for it. I was praised by the most lily-white men of the town. I was considered an example of desirable conduct—just as my grandfather had been. And what puzzled me was that the old man had defined it as treachery. When I was praised for my conduct I felt a guilt that in some way I was doing something that was really against the wishes of the white folks, that if they had understood they would have desired me to act just the opposite, that I should have been sulky and mean, and that that really would have been what they wanted, even though they were fooled and thought they wanted me to act as I did. It made me afraid that some day they would look upon me as a traitor and I would be lost. Still I was more afraid to act any other way because they didn't like that at all. The old man's words were like a curse. On my graduation day I delivered an oration in which I showed that humility was the secret, indeed, the very essence of progress. (Not that I believed this—how could I, remembering my grandfather?—I only believed that it worked.) It was a great success. Everyone praised me and I was invited to give the speech at a gathering of the town's leading white citizens. It was a triumph for our whole community.

It was in the main ballroom of the leading hotel. When I got there I discovered that it was on the occasion of a smoker, and I was told that since I was to be there anyway I might as well take part in the battle royal to be fought by some of my schoolmates as part of the entertainment. The battle royal came first.

All of the town's big shots were there in their tuxedoes, wolfing down the buffet foods, drinking beer and whiskey and smoking black cigars. It was a large room with a high ceiling. Chairs were arranged in neat rows around three sides of a portable boxing ring. The fourth side was clear, revealing a gleaming space of polished floor. I had some misgivings over the battle royal, by the way. Not from a distaste for fighting, but because I didn't care too much for the other fellows who were to take part. They were tough guys who seemed to have no grandfather's curse worrying their minds. No one could mistake their toughness. And besides, I suspected that fighting a battle royal might detract from the dignity of my speech. In those pre-invisible days I visualized myself as a potential Booker T. Washington. But the other fellows didn't care too much for me either, and there were nine of them. I felt superior to them in my way, and I didn't like the manner in which we were all crowded together into the servants' elevator. Nor did they like my being there. In fact, as the warmly lighted floors flashed past the elevator we had words over the fact that I, by taking part in the fight, had knocked one of their friends out of a night's work.

We were led out of the elevator through a rococo hall into an anteroom and told to get into our fighting togs. Each of us was issued a pair of boxing gloves and ushered out into the big mirrored hall, which we entered looking cautiously about us and whispering, lest we might accidentally be heard above the noise of the room. It was foggy with cigar smoke. And already the whiskey was taking effect. I was shocked to see some of the most important men of the town quite tipsy. They were all there—bankers, lawyers, judges, doctors, fire chiefs, teachers, merchants. Even one of the more fashionable pastors. Something we could not see was going on up front. A clarinet was vibrating sensuously and the men were standing up and moving eagerly forward. We were a small tight group, clustered together, our bare upper bodies touching and shining with anticipatory sweat, while up front the big shots were becoming increasingly excited over something we still could not see. Suddenly I heard the school superintendent, who had told me to come, yell, "Bring up the shines, gentlemen! Bring up the little shines!"

We were rushed up to the front of the ballroom, where it smelled even more strongly of tobacco and whiskey. Then we were pushed into place. I almost wet my pants. A sea of faces, some hostile, some amused, ringed around us, and in the center, facing us, stood a magnificent blonde—stark naked. There was dead silence. I felt a blast of cold air chill me. I tried to back away, but they were behind me and around me. Some of the boys stood with lowered heads, trembling. I felt a wave of irrational guilt and fear. My teeth chattered, my skin turned to goose flesh, my knees knocked. Yet I was strongly attracted and looked in spite of myself. Had the price of looking been blindness,

I would have looked. The hair was yellow like that of a circus kewpie doll, the face heavily powdered and rouged, as though to form an abstract mask, the eyes hollow and smeared a cool blue, the color of a baboon's butt. I felt a desire to spit upon her as my eyes brushed slowly over her body. Her breasts were firm and round as the domes of East Indian temples, and I stood so close as to see the fine skin texture and beads of pearly perspiration glistening like dew around the pink and erected buds of her nipples. I wanted at one and the same time to run from the room, to sink through the floor, or go to her and cover her from my eyes and the eyes of the others with my body; to feel the soft thighs, to caress her and destroy her, to love her and murder her, to hide from her, and yet to stroke where below the small American flag tattooed upon her belly her thighs formed a capital V. I had a notion that of all in the room she saw only me with her impersonal eyes.

And then she began to dance, a slow sensuous movement; the smoke of a hundred cigars clinging to her like the thinnest of veils. She seemed like a fair bird-girl girdled in veils calling to me from the angry surface of some gray and threatening sea. I was transported. Then I became aware of the clarinet playing and the big shots yelling at us. Some threatened us if we looked and others if we did not. On my right I saw one boy faint. And now a man grabbed a silver pitcher from a table and stepped close as he dashed ice water upon him and stood him up and forced two of us to support him as his head hung and moans issued from his thick bluish lips. Another boy began to plead to go home. He was the largest of the group, wearing dark red fighting trunks much too small to conceal the erection which projected from him as though in answer to the insinuating low-registered moaning of the clarinet. He tried to hide himself with his boxing gloves.

And all the while the blonde continued dancing, smiling faintly at the big shots who watched her with fascination, and faintly smiling at our fear. I noticed a certain merchant who followed her hungrily, his lips loose and drooling. He was a large man who wore diamond studs in a shirtfront which swelled with the ample paunch underneath, and each time the blonde swayed her undulating hips he ran his hand through the thin hair of his bald head and, with his arms upheld, his posture clumsy like that of an intoxicated panda, wound his belly in a slow and obscene grind. This creature was completely hypnotized. The music had quickened. As the dancer flung herself about with a detached expression on her face, the men began reaching out to touch her. I could see their beefy fingers sink into the soft flesh. Some of the others tried to stop them and she began to move around the floor in graceful circles, as they gave chase, slipping and sliding over the polished floor. It was mad. Chairs went crashing, drinks were spilt, as they ran laughing and howling after her. They caught her just as she reached a door, raised her from the floor, and tossed her as college boys are tossed at a hazing, and above her red, fixed-smiling lips I saw the terror and disgust in her eyes, almost like my own terror and that which I saw in some of the other boys. As I watched, they tossed her twice and her soft breasts seemed to flatten against the air and her legs flung wildly as she spun. Some of the more sober ones helped her to escape. And I started off the floor, heading for the anteroom with the rest of the boys.

Some were still crying and in hysteria. But as we tried to leave we were stopped and ordered to get into the ring. There was nothing to do but what we were told. All ten of us climbed under the ropes and allowed ourselves to be blindfolded with broad bands of white cloth. One of the men seemed to feel a bit sympathetic and tried to cheer us up as we stood with our backs against the ropes. Some of us tried to grin. "See that boy over there?" one of the men said. "I want you to run across at the bell and give it to him right in the belly. If you don't get him, I'm going to get you. I don't like his looks." Each of us was told the same. The blindfolds were put on. Yet even then I had been going over my speech. In my mind each word was as bright as flame. I felt the cloth pressed into place, and frowned so that it would be loosened when I relaxed.

But now I felt a sudden fit of blind terror. I was unused to darkness. It was as though I had suddenly found myself in a dark room filled with poisonous cottonmouths. I could hear the bleary voices yelling insistently for the battle royal to begin.

"Get going in there!"

"Let me at the big nigger!"

I strained to pick up the school superintendent's voice, as though to squeeze some security out of that slightly more familiar sound.

"Let me at those black sonsabitches!" someone yelled.

"No, Jackson, no!" another voice yelled. "Here, somebody, help me hold Jack."

"I want to get at that ginger-colored nigger. Tear him limb from limb," the first voice yelled.

I stood against the ropes trembling. For in those days I was what they called ginger-colored, and he sounded as though he might crunch me between his teeth like a crisp ginger cookie.

Quite a struggle was going on. Chairs were being kicked about and I could hear voices grunting as with a terrific effort. I wanted to see, to see more desperately than ever before. But the blindfold was as tight as a thick skin-puckering scab and when I raised my gloved hands to push the layers of white aside a voice yelled, "Oh, no you don't, black bastard! Leave that alone!"

"Ring the bell before Jackson kills him a coon!" someone boomed in the sudden silence. And I heard the bell clang and the sound of the feet scuffling forward.

A glove smacked against my head. I pivoted, striking out stiffly as someone went past, and felt the jar ripple along the length of my arm to my shoulder. Then it seemed as though all nine of the boys had turned upon me at once. Blows pounded me from all sides while I struck out as best I could. So many blows landed upon me that I wondered if I were not the only blindfolded fighter in the ring, or if the man called Jackson hadn't succeeded in getting me after all.

Blindfolded, I could no longer control my motions. I had no dignity. I stumbled about like a baby or a drunken man. The smoke had become thicker and with each new blow it seemed to sear and further restrict my lungs. My saliva became like hot bitter glue. A glove connected with my head, filling my mouth with warm blood. It was everywhere. I could not tell if the moisture I felt upon my body was sweat or blood. A blow landed hard against the nape of my neck. I felt myself going over, my head hitting the floor. Streaks of blue light filled the black world behind the blindfold. I lay prone, pretending that I was knocked out, but felt myself seized by hands and yanked to my feet. "Get going, black boy! Mix it up!" My arms were like lead, my head smarting from blows. I managed to feel my way to the ropes and held on, trying to catch my breath. A glove landed in my midsection and I went over again, feeling as though the smoke had become a knife jabbed into my guts. Pushed this way and that by the legs milling around me, I finally pulled erect and discovered that I could see the black, sweat-washed forms weaving in the smoky-blue atmosphere like drunken dancers weaving to the rapid drum-like thuds of blows.

Everyone fought hysterically. It was complete anarchy. Everybody fought everybody else. No group fought together for long. Two,

three, four, fought one, then turned to fight each other, were themselves attacked. Blows landed below the belt and in the kidney, with
the gloves open as well as closed, and with my eye partly opened now
there was not so much terror. I moved carefully, avoiding blows, although not too many to attract attention, fighting from group to group.
The boys groped about like blind, cautious crabs crouching to protect
their mid-sections, their heads pulled in short against their shoulders,
their arms stretched nervously before them, with their fists testing the
smoke-filled air like the knobbed feelers of hypersensitive snails. In
one corner I glimpsed a boy violently punching the air and heard him
scream in pain as he smashed his hand against a ring post. For a second I saw him bent over holding his hand, then going down as a blow
caught his unprotected head. I played one group against the other, slipping in and throwing a punch then stepping out of range while pushing
the others into the melee to take the blows blindly aimed at me. The
smoke was agonizing and there were no rounds, no bells at three minute
intervals to relieve our exhaustion. The room spun round me, a swirl
of lights, smoke, sweating bodies surrounded by tense white faces. I
bled from both nose and mouth, the blood spattering upon my chest.

The men kept yelling, "Slug him, black boy! Knock his guts out!"

"Uppercut him! Kill him! Kill that big boy!"

Taking a fake fall, I saw a boy going down heavily beside me as
though we were felled by a single blow, saw a sneaker-clad foot shoot
into his groin as the two who had knocked him down stumbled upon
him. I rolled out of range, feeling a twinge of nausea.

The harder we fought the more threatening the men became. And
yet, I had begun to worry about my speech again. How would it go?
Would they recognize my ability? What would they give me?

I was fighting automatically when suddenly I noticed that one after
another of the boys was leaving the ring. I was surprised, filled with
panic, as though I had been left alone with an unknown danger. Then
I understood. The boys had arranged it among themselves. It was the
custom for the two men left in the ring to slug it out for the winner's
prize. I discovered this too late. When the bell sounded two men in
tuxedos leaped into the ring and removed the blindfold. I found myself
facing Tatlock, the biggest of the gang. I felt sick at my stomach.
Hardly had the bell stopped ringing in my ears than it clanged again
and I saw him moving swiftly toward me. Thinking of nothing else to
do I hit him smash on the nose. He kept coming, bringing the rank

sharp violence of stale sweat. His face was a black blank of a face, only his eyes alive—with hate of me and aglow with a feverish terror from what had happened to us all. I became anxious. I wanted to deliver my speech and he came at me as though he meant to beat it out of me. I smashed him again and again, taking his blows as they came. Then on a sudden impulse I struck him lightly and as we clinched, I whispered "Fake like I knocked you out, you can have the prize."

"I'll break your behind," he whispered hoarsely.

"For *them*?"

"For *me*, sonofabitch."

They were yelling for us to break it up and Tatlock spun me half around with a blow, and as a joggled camera sweeps in a reeling scene, I saw the howling red faces crouching tense beneath the cloud of blue-gray smoke. For a moment the world wavered, unraveled, flowed, then my head cleared and Tatlock bounced before me. That fluttering shadow before my eyes was his jabbing left hand. Then falling forward, my head against his damp shoulder, I whispered,

"I'll make it five dollars more."

"Go to hell!"

But his muscles relaxed a trifle beneath my pressure and I breathed, "Seven?"

"Give it to your ma," he said, ripping me beneath the heart. And while I still held him I butted him and moved away. I felt myself bombarded with punches. I fought back with hopeless desperation. I wanted to deliver my speech more than anything else in the world because I felt that only these men could judge truly my ability, and now this stupid clown was ruining my chances. I began fighting carefully now, moving in to punch him and out again with my greater speed. A lucky blow to his chin and I had him going too—until I heard a loud voice yell, "I got my money on the big boy."

Hearing this, I almost dropped my guard. I was confused: Should I try to win against the voice out there? Would not this go against my speech, and was not this a moment for humility, for nonresistance? A blow to my head as I danced about sent my right eye popping like a jack-in-the-box and settled my dilemma. The room went red as I fell. It was a dream fall, my body languid and fastidious as to where to land, until the floor became impatient and smashed up to meet me. A moment later I came to. An hypnotic voice said FIVE emphatically.

And I lay there, hazily watching a dark red spot of my own blood shaping itself into a butterfly, glistening and soaking into the soiled gray world of the canvas.

When the voice drawled TEN I was lifted up and dragged to a chair. I sat dazed. My eye pained and swelled with each throb of my pounding heart and I wondered if now I would be allowed to speak. I was wringing wet, my mouth still bleeding. We were grouped along the wall now. The other boys ignored me as they congratulated Tatlock and speculated as to how much they would be paid. One boy whimpered over his smashed hand. Looking up front, I saw attendants in white jackets rolling the portable ring away and placing a small square rug in the vacant space surrounded by chairs. Perhaps, I thought, I will stand on the rug to deliver my speech.

Then the M.C. called to us, "Come on up here boys and get your money."

We ran forward to where the men laughed and talked in their chairs, waiting. Everyone seemed friendly now.

"There it is on the rug," the man said. I saw the rug covered with coins of all dimensions and a few crumpled bills. But what excited me, scattered here and there, were the gold pieces.

"Boys, it's all yours," the man said. "You get all you grab."

"That's right, Sambo," a blond man said, winking at me confidentially.

I trembled with excitement, forgetting my pain. I would get the gold and the bills, I thought. I would use both hands. I would throw my body against the boys nearest me to block them from the gold.

"Get down around the rug now," the man commanded, "and don't anyone touch it until I give the signal."

"This ought to be good," I heard.

As told, we got around the square rug on our knees. Slowly the man raised his freckled hand as we followed it upward with our eyes.

I heard, "These niggers look like they're about to pray!"

Then, "Ready," the man said. "Go!"

I lunged for a yellow coin lying on the blue design of the carpet, touching it and sending a surprised shriek to join those rising around me. I tried frantically to remove my hand but could not let go. A hot, violent force tore through my body, shaking me like a wet rat. The rug was electrified. The hair bristled up on my head as I shook myself free. My muscles jumped, my nerves jangled, writhed. But I saw that this was not stopping the other boys. Laughing in fear and embarrassment, some were holding back and scooping up the coins knocked off by the painful contortions of the others. The men roared above us as we struggled.

"Pick it up, goddamnit, pick it up!" someone called like a bass-voiced parrot. "Go on, get it!"

I crawled rapidly around the floor, picking up the coins trying to avoid the coppers and to get greenbacks and the gold. Ignoring the shock by laughing, as I brushed the coins off quickly, I discovered that I could contain the electricity—a contradiction, but it works. Then the men began to push us onto the rug. Laughing embarrassedly, we struggled out of their hands and kept after the coins. We were all wet and slippery and hard to hold. Suddenly I saw a boy lifted into the air, glistening with sweat like a circus seal, and dropped, his wet back landing flush upon the charged rug, heard him yell and saw him literally dance upon his back, his elbows beating a frenzied tattoo upon the floor, his muscles twitching like the flesh of a horse stung by many flies. When he finally rolled off, his face was gray and no one stopped him when he ran from the floor amid booming laughter.

"Get the money," the M.C. called. "That's good hard American cash!"

And we snatched and grabbed, snatched and grabbed. I was careful not to come too close to the rug now, and when I felt the hot whiskey breath descend upon me like a cloud of foul air I reached out and grabbed the leg of a chair. It was occupied and I held on desperately.

"Leggo nigger! Leggo!"

The huge face wavered down to mine as he tried to push me free. But my body was slippery and he was too drunk. It was Mr. Colcord, who owned a chain of movie houses and "entertainment palaces." Each time he grabbed me I slipped out of his hands. It became a real struggle. I feared the rug more than I did the drunk, so I held on, surprising myself for a moment by trying to topple *him* upon the rug. It was such an enormous idea that I found myself actually carrying it out. I tried not to be obvious, yet when I grabbed his leg, trying to tumble him out of the chair, he raised up roaring with laughter, and, looking at me with soberness dead in the eye, kicked me viciously in the chest. The chair leg flew out of my hand and I felt myself going and rolled. It was as though I had rolled through a bed of hot coals. It seemed a whole century would pass before I would roll free, a century in which I was seared through the deepest levels of my body to the fearful breath within me and the breath seared and heated to the point of explosion. It'll all be over in a flash, I thought as I rolled clear. It'll all be over in a flash.

But not yet, the men on the other side were waiting, red faces swollen as though from apoplexy as they bent forward in their chairs. Seeing their fingers coming toward me I rolled away as a fumbled football rolls off the receiver's fingertips, back into the coals. That time I luckily sent the rug sliding out of place and heard the coins ringing against the floor and the boys scuffling to pick them up and the M.C. calling, "All right, boys, that's all. Go get dressed and get your money."

I was limp as a dish rag. My back felt as though it had been beaten with wires.

When we had dressed the M.C. came in and gave us each five dollars, except Tatlock, who got ten for being last in the ring. Then he told us to leave. I was not to get a chance to deliver my speech, I thought. I was going out into the dim alley in despair when I was stopped and told to go back. I returned to the ballroom, where the men were pushing back their chairs and gathering in groups to talk.

The M.C. knocked on a table for quiet. "Gentlemen," he said, "we almost forgot an important part of the program. A most serious part, gentlemen. This boy was brought here to deliver a speech which he made at his graduation yesterday . . . "

"Bravo!"

"I'm told that he is the smartest boy we've got out there in Greenwood. I'm told that he knows more big words than a pocket-sized dictionary."

Much applause and laughter.

"So now, gentlemen, I want you to give him your attention."

There was still laughter as I faced them, my mouth dry, my eye throbbing. I began slowly, but evidently my throat was tense, because they began shouting, "Louder! Louder!"

"We of the younger generation extol the wisdom of that great leader and educator," I shouted, "who first spoke these flaming words of wisdom: 'A ship lost at sea for many days suddenly sighted a friendly vessel. From the mast of the unfortunate vessel was seen a signal: "Water, water; we die of thirst!" The answer from the friendly vessel came back: "Cast down your bucket where you are." The captain of the distressed vessel, at last heeding the injunction, cast down his bucket, and it came up full of fresh sparkling water from the mouth of the Amazon River.' And like him I say, and in his words, 'To those of my race who depend upon bettering their condition in a foreign land, or who underestimate the importance of cultivating friendly relations with the Southern white man, who is his next-door neighbor, I would say: "Cast down your bucket where you are"—cast it down in making friends in every manly way of the people of all races by whom we are surrounded . . . ' "

I spoke automatically and with such fervor that I did not realize that the men were still talking and laughing until my dry mouth, filling up with blood from the cut, almost strangled me. I coughed, wanting to stop and go to one of the tall brass, sandfilled spittoons to relieve myself, but a few of the men, especially the superintendent, were listening and I was afraid. So I gulped it down, blood, saliva and all, and continued. (What powers of endurance I had during those days! What enthusiasm! What a belief in the rightness of things!) I spoke even louder in spite of the pain. But still they talked and still they laughed, as though deaf with cotton in dirty ears. So I spoke with greater emotional emphasis. I closed my ears and swallowed blood until I was nauseated. The speech seemed a hundred times as long as before, but I could not leave out a single word. All had to be said, each memorized nuance considered, rendered. Nor was that all. Whenever I uttered a word of three or more syllables a group of voices would yell for me to repeat it. I used the phrase "social responsibility" and they yelled:

"What's that word you say, boy?"

"Social responsibility," I said.

"What?"

"Social . . . "

"Louder."

" . . . responsibility."

"More!"

"Respon—"

"Repeat!"

"—sibility."

The room filled with the uproar of laughter until, no doubt, distracted by having to gulp down my blood, I made a mistake and yelled a phrase I had often seen denounced in newspaper editorials, heard debated in private.

"Social . . . "

"What?" they yelled.

" . . . equality—"

The laughter hung smokelike in the sudden stillness. I opened my eyes, puzzled. Sounds of displeasure filled the room. The M.C. rushed forward. They shouted hostile phrases at me. But I did not understand.

A small dry mustached man in the front row blared out, "Say that slowly, son!"

"What sir?"

"What you just said!"

"Social responsibility, sir," I said.

"You weren't being smart, were you, boy?" he said, not unkindly.

"No, sir!"

"You sure that about 'equality' was a mistake?"

"Oh, yes, sir," I said. "I was swallowing blood."

"Well, you had better speak more slowly so we can understand. We mean to do right by you, but you've got to know your place at all times. All right, now, go on with your speech."

I was afraid. I wanted to leave but I wanted also to speak and I was afraid they'd snatch me down.

"Thank you, sir," I said, beginning where I had left off, and having them ignore me as before.

Yet when I finished there was a thunderous applause. I was surprised to see the superintendent come forth with a package wrapped in white tissue paper, and, gesturing for quiet, address the men.

"Gentlemen, you see that I did not overpraise this boy. He makes a good speech and some day he'll lead his people in the proper paths. And I don't have to tell you that that is important in these days and times. This is a good, smart boy, and so to encourage him in the right direction, in the name of the Board of Education I wish to present him a prize in the form of this . . . "

He paused, removing the tissue paper and revealing a gleaming calfskin brief case.

" . . . in the form of this first-class article from Shad Whitmore's shop."

"Boy," he said, addressing me, "take this prize and keep it well. Consider it a badge of office. Prize it. Keep developing as you are and some day it will be filled with important papers that will help shape the destiny of your people."

I was so moved that I could hardly express my thanks. A rope of bloody saliva forming a shape like an undiscovered continent drooled upon the leather and I wiped it quickly away. I felt an importance that I had never dreamed.

"Open it and see what's inside," I was told.

My fingers a-tremble, I complied, smelling the fresh leather and finding an official-looking document inside. It was a scholarship to the state College for Negroes. My eyes filled with tears and I ran awkwardly off the floor.

I was overjoyed; I did not even mind when I discovered that the gold pieces I had scrambled for were brass pocket tokens advertising a certain make of automobile. When I reached home everyone was excited. Next day the neighbors came to congratulate me. I even felt safe from grandfather, whose deathbed curse usually spoiled my triumphs. I stood beneath his photograph with my brief case in hand and smiled triumphantly into his stolid black peasant's face. It was a face that fascinated me. The eyes seemed to follow everywhere I went.

That night I dreamed I was at a circus with him and that he refused to laugh at the clowns no matter what they did. Then later he told me to open my brief case and read what was inside and I did, finding an official envelope stamped with the state seal; and inside the envelope I found another and another, endlessly, and I thought I would fall of weariness. "Them's years," he said. "Now open that one." And I did and in it I found an engraved document containing a short message in letters of gold. "Read it," my grandfather said. "Out loud."

"To Whom It May Concern," I intoned. "Keep This Nigger-Boy Running."

I awoke with the old man's laughter ringing in my ears.

(It was a dream I was to remember and dream again for many years after. But at that time I had no insight into its meaning. First I had to attend college.)

3

MISS BRILL
by Katherine Mansfield

Although it was so brilliantly fine—the blue sky powdered with gold and great spots of light like white wine splashed over the Jardins Publiques—Miss Brill was glad that she had decided on her fur. The air was motionless, but when you opened your mouth there was just a faint chill, like a chill from a glass of iced water before you sip, and now and again a leaf came drifting—from nowhere, from the sky. Miss Brill put up her hand and touched her fur. Dear little thing. It was nice to feel it again. She had taken it out of its box that afternoon, shaken out the moth-powder, given it a good brush, and rubbed the life back into the dim little eyes. "What has been happening to me?" said the sad little eyes. Oh, how sweet it was to see them snap at her again from the red eiderdown!... But the nose, which was of some black composition, wasn't at all firm. It must have had a knock, somehow. Never mind—a little dab of black sealing-wax when the time came—when it was absolutely necessary.... Little rogue! Yes, she really felt like that about it. Little rogue biting its tail just by her left ear. She could have taken it off and laid it on her lap and stroked it. She felt a tingling in her hands and arms, but that came from walking, she supposed. And when she breathed, something light and sad—no, not sad, exactly—something gentle seemed to move in her bosom.

There were a number of people out this afternoon, far more than last Sunday. And the band sounded louder and gayer. That was because the Season had begun. For although the band played all the year round on Sundays, out of season it was never the same. It was like some one playing with only the family to listen; it didn't care how it played if there weren't any strangers present. Wasn't the conductor wearing a new coat, too? She was sure it was new. He scraped with his foot and flapped his arms like a rooster about to crow, and the bandsmen sitting in the green rotunda blew out their cheeks and glared at the music. Now there came a little "flutey" bit—very pretty!—a little chain of bright drops. She was sure it would be repeated. It was; she lifted her head and smiled.

Only two people shared her "special" seat: a fine old man in a velvet coat, his hands clasped over a huge carved walking-stick, and a big old woman, sitting upright, with a roll of knitting on her embroidered apron. They did not speak. This was disappointing, for Miss Brill always looked forward to the conversation. She had become really quite expert, she thought, at listening as though she didn't listen, at sitting in other people's lives just for a minute while they talked round her.

She glanced, sideways, at the old couple. Perhaps they would go soon. Last Sunday, too, hadn't been as interesting as usual. An Englishman and his wife, he wearing a dreadful Panama hat and she button boots. And she'd gone on the whole time about how she ought to wear spectacles; she knew she needed them; but that it was no good getting any; they'd be sure to break and they'd never keep on. And he'd been so patient. He'd suggested everything–gold rims, the kind that curved round your ears, little pads inside the bridge. No, nothing would please her. "They'll always be sliding down my nose!" Miss Brill had wanted to shake her.

The old people sat on the bench, still as statues. Never mind, there was always the crowd to watch. To and fro, in front of the flower-beds and the band rotunda, the couples and groups paraded, stopped to talk, to greet, to buy a handful of flowers from the old beggar who had his tray fixed to the railings. Little children ran among them, swooping and laughing; little boys with big white silk bows under their chins, little girls, little French dolls, dressed up in velvet and lace. And sometimes a tiny staggerer came suddenly rocking into the open from under the trees, stopped, stared, as suddenly sat down "flop," until its small high-stepping mother, like a young hen, rushed scolding to its rescue. Other people sat on the benches and green chairs, but they were nearly always the same, Sunday after Sunday, and—Miss Brill had often noticed—there was something funny about nearly all of them. They were odd, silent, nearly all old, and from the way they stared they looked as though they'd just come from dark little rooms or even—even cupboards!

Behind the rotunda the slender trees with yellow leaves down drooping, and through them just a line of sea, and beyond the blue sky with gold-veined clouds.

Tum-tum-tum tiddle-um! tiddle-um! tum tiddley-um tum ta! blew the band.

Two young girls in red came by and two young soldiers in blue met them, and they laughed and paired and went off arm-in-arm. Two peasant women with funny straw hats passed, gravely, leading beautiful smoke-coloured donkeys. A cold, pale nun hurried by. A beautiful woman came along and dropped her bunch of violets, and a little boy ran after to hand them to her, and she took them and threw them away as if they'd been poisoned. Dear me! Miss Brill didn't know whether to admire that or not! And now an ermine toque and a gentleman in grey met just in front of her. He was tall, stiff, dignified, and she was wearing the ermine toque she'd bought when her hair was yellow. Now everything, her hair, her face, even her eyes, was the same colour as the shabby ermine, and her hand, in its cleaned glove, lifted to dab her lips, was a tiny yellowish paw. Oh, she was so pleased to see him—delighted! She rather thought they were going to meet that afternoon. She described where she'd been—everywhere, here, there, along by the sea. The day was so charming—didn't he agree? And wouldn't he, perhaps? . . . But he shook his head, lighted a cigarette, slowly breathed a great deep puff into her face, and, even while she was still talking and laughing, flicked the match away and walked on. The ermine toque was alone; she smiled more brightly than ever. But even the band seemed to know what she was feeling and played more softly, played tenderly, and the drum beat, "The Brute! The Brute!" over and over. What would she do? What was going to happen now? But as Miss Brill wondered, the ermine toque turned, raised her hand as though she'd seen some one else much nicer, just over there, and pattered away. And the band changed again and played more quickly, more gaily than ever, and the old couple on Miss Brill's seat got up and marched away, and such a funny old man with long whiskers hobbled along in time to the music and was nearly knocked over by four girls walking abreast.

Oh, how fascinating it was! How she enjoyed it! How she loved sitting here, watching it all! It was like a play. It was exactly like a play. Who could believe the sky at the back wasn't painted? But it wasn't till a little brown dog trotted on solemn and then slowly trotted off, like a little "theatre" dog, a little dog that had been drugged, that Miss Brill discovered what it was that made it so exciting. They were all on the stage. They weren't only the audience, not only looking on; they were acting. Even she had a part and came every Sunday. No doubt somebody would have noticed if she hadn't been there; she was part of the performance after all. How strange she'd never thought of it like that before! And yet it explained why she made such a point of starting from home at just the same time each week—so as not to be late for the performance—and it also explained why she had quite a queer, shy feeling at telling her English pupils how she spent her Sunday afternoons. No wonder! Miss Brill nearly laughed out loud. She was on the stage. She thought of the old invalid gentleman to whom she read the newspaper four afternoons a week while he slept in the garden. She had got quite used to the frail head on the cotton pillow, the hollowed eyes, the open mouth and the high pinched nose. If he'd been dead she mightn't have noticed for weeks; she wouldn't have minded. But suddenly he knew he was having the paper read to him by an actress! "An actress!" The old head lifted; two points of light quivered in the old eyes. "An actress—are ye?" And Miss Brill smoothed the newspaper as though it were the manuscript of her part and said gently: "Yes, I have been an actress for a long time."

The band had been having a rest. Now they started again. And what they played was warm, sunny, yet there was just a faint chill—a something, what was it?—not sadness—no, not sadness—a something that made you want to sing. The tune lifted, lifted, the light shone; and it seemed to Miss Brill that in another moment all of them, all the whole company, would begin singing. The young ones, the laughing ones who were moving together, they would begin, and the men's voices, very resolute and brave, would join them. And then she too, she too, and the others on the benches—they would come in with a kind of accompaniment—something low, that scarcely rose or fell, something so beautiful—moving . . . . And Miss Brill's eyes filled with tears and she looked smiling at all the other members of the company. Yes, we understand, we understand, she thought—though what they understood she didn't know.

Just at that moment a boy and a girl came and sat down where the old couple had been. They were beautifully dressed; they were in love. The hero and heroine, of course, just arrived from his father's yacht. And still soundlessly singing, still with that trembling smile, Miss Brill prepared to listen.

"No, not now," said the girl. "Not here, I can't."

"But why? Because of that stupid old thing at the end there?" asked the boy. "Why does she come here at all—who wants her? Why doesn't she keep her silly old mug at home?"

"It's her fu-fur which is so funny," giggled the girl. "It's exactly like a fried whiting"

"Ah, be off with you!" said the boy in an angry whisper. Then: "Tell me, ma petite chere–"

"No, not here," said the girl. "Not yet."

On her way home she usually bought a slice of honey-cake at the baker's. It was her Sunday treat. Sometimes there was an almond in her slice, sometimes not. It made a great difference. If there was an almond it was like carrying home a tiny present–a surprise–something that might very well not have been there. She hurried on the almond Sundays and struck the match for the kettle in quite a dashing way.

But to-day she passed the baker's by, climbed the stairs, went into the little dark room—her room like a cupboard—and sat down on the red eiderdown. She sat there for a long time. The box that the fur came out of was on the bed. She unclasped the necklet quickly; quickly, without looking, laid it inside. But when she put the lid on she thought she heard something crying .

4
EMOTIONAL, IMAGINATIVE, AND INTELLECTUAL RESPONSES TO FICTION

Everything a writer does in the creative process is meant to evoke a response from you. Writers are not *conscious* as they write of everything they are doing that will affect the reader; the *unconscious* plays a major role in the creative process. Just as there is no way to account exactly for the formation of strange images in your dreams, the unconscious shapes stories long before the writer begins the conscious process of writing.

And as the writer's past emotional, imaginative, and intellectual experiences determine what and how he or she writes, your past experiences determine how you respond as a reader to a story. Whatever the writer consciously or unconsciously produces in the story, your own responses will be both conscious and unconscious. But because the writer and the reader have universal experiences in common, what the writer writes and what the reader reads come so close that a room full of students can discuss that story profitably.

One way to see the role of the teacher is as a mediator between the writer and the reader as student.

Most writers intend, line by line, first to stimulate your emotions and in doing so to stimulate your imagination, followed by some sort of intellectual reassessment. It is of major importance to stress that ideally all three kinds of experiences happen simultaneously, but that there will be an emphasis at any given point, or generally in any given story, on one. For instance, in "Miss Brill," the general focus is on emotion; readers feel with and for Miss Brill. In "A Good Man Is Hard to Find," the general emphasis is on readers' intellects as they "judge" the behavior of the family members. But given the foreshadowing about the Misfit, and certainly after the appearance of the car, readers' imaginations are activated; they imagine what can happen. In "Battle Royal," the emphasis in the opening is upon the intellect; the narrator is reassessing his life; once the fight begins, the emphasis shifts to the emotional impact. Ellison controls the fight so carefully, the reader's imagination is not particularly stimulated.

One purpose of this handbook is to show ways writers employ a wide range of techniques to affect you, the reader, emotionally, imaginatively, and intellectually. Through the choice of *point of view*, the writer controls all the other elements in the work of fiction and thus intensifies your responses. You will learn how point of view determines *style;* how point of view and style create *contexts*; and how contexts generate *implications*. These terms are defined, with examples, in the chapter on techniques.

5

SOME DIFFERENCES BETWEEN COMMERCIAL AND LITERARY FICTION

When we talk about reading fiction, it is sobering to bear this fact in mind: only about three percent of the adult population reads more than one book of any type each year. Most readers of fiction read genre fiction: historical or gothic romance, science fiction, detective, spy, western, occult, contemporary love stories, or best-sellers that center upon a subject—for example, sharks (*Jaws*), the mafia (*The Godfather*), the occult (*The Exorcist*). Such fiction is called "formula" or "commercial" as opposed to "serious" or "literary." No reader need be defensive or apologetic about liking or even preferring commercial fiction. Some readers enjoy both literary and popular fiction.

Over the past two decades, studies in popular culture have clearly shown that a study of commercial fiction may provide a kind of sociological understanding of mass culture. Few readers of commercial fiction, however, are aware of such insights.

The terms "commercial" and "literary" run the risk all labels do of distorting. Here, they are used to describe, not to evaluate. Readers may make value judgments about which type is better, or more useful, or artistic. But perhaps the most useful way to look at the question, in this *study* situation, is to agree that commercial and literary fiction offer *different* kinds of experiences and to describe some of those differences. The analytical question is: How do you account for these variations? In evaluating both types, consider what each sets out to achieve. Ask yourself, "How does each story do what it does to the reader?"

By temperament or by conscious strategy, commercial or popular writers strive for immediate effects, knowing most of their readers are looking for a "good story" that will provide instant gratification for an already passing desire for diversion, entertainment, or escape. They have fixed assumptions about their likely readers and manipulate as immediately and effectively as possible their attitudes and expectations. They skillfully employ devices that get predictable responses. The opening paragraphs of formula stories attempt to accost readers with a tug of the sleeve as they pass. Formula fiction offers readers characters with whom they can easily identify; a simple plot or story line that produces a clearly posed conflict, a rapid pace, violent action, suspense, demure or graphic sex scenes, and a happy or "neat" ending; and a moral or message that is "easy" to comprehend.

Though literary writers may think less consciously of *who* their readers may be, they do take great care to create effects to which they expect attentive readers to respond. The three writers whose stories you have just read assume that you are a sensitive, imaginative, intelligent collaborator in the creative process; that you expect, even require, them to make demands on you; and that you expect to derive, perhaps through several readings, a lasting spiritual, esthetic, intellectual pleasure from every aspect of the experiences they have created for you.

Commercial types of stories are conceived to appeal to the tastes of the general reader, and to entertain. If entertainment is the commercial writer's sole or main purpose, it doesn't matter very much why or how he or she achieves that purpose. But the serious writer wants both to entertain and to enlighten. Readers require of commercial fiction that it take them out of the life they know into a life they imagine they would prefer; readers of literary fiction turn to fiction because it subjects them more intensely than experience iteself does to the world we actually live in. If commercial fiction offers a vicarious escape from the limitations of our lives in this world, literary fiction increases our understanding of those limitations and sharpens our awareness of that world. The term realism, however, does not always apply to serious fiction, which may employ fantasy.

Readers of commercial or formula fiction ask, "But why are serious stories often so unpleasant?" One of the purposes of serious fiction is to interpret life. The writer observes that human nature and experience are complex, chaotic, sometimes senseless. The truth as the writer perceives it may strike readers who turn to fiction for reassurance as disturbing. "Life is depressing enough as it is," such readers often declare. What those readers have not yet experienced is the special pleasure and excitement that comes with self-discovery and self-understanding.

Confronted with serious or literary fiction in the classroom—or in social situations—most readers declare, "I read for pleasure or escape, not for intellectual reasons." Thematic emphases in discussions of fiction give the impression that the main purpose of literary fiction is to illustrate philosophical propositions. That is a common misunderstanding. Most readers who study fiction discover that *the particular pleasure* literary fiction provides is derived from a complex presentation of character, setting, plot, conflict, even sex and violence—with a different use of suspense, action, pace—through techniques that are as distinctively imagined as the story elements themselves. The meaning may be more difficult to "grasp," but there is a pleasure in experiencing *thought*, suffused with emotion and imagination, that one can have nowhere else but in reading literary fiction.

6

SOME PARALLELS BETWEEN THE ACT OF WRITING FICTION AND THE ACT OF READING FICTION

One way to achieve an understanding of the nature and concepts of fiction and to appreciate its effects is to have in mind some sense of how the creative process works.

Let's imagine a writer who is willing to describe to you why and how she or he writes. That writer might say, "In the writing process, *I* experience what I *imagine* the character and the reader are experiencing *with* me.

"There are three dimensions to that experience, for me, for the character, and for the reader: emotion, imagination, and intellect.

"How do I do that to you? I use two major techniques—*point of view* and *style*—to create *contexts*, which generate *implications* in such a way that the experience of reading the story never ends." (See chapter on techniques for definitions of these terms.)

The commercial writer, by contrast, also enjoys the writing process, but writes mainly to make money. The reader's experience is mainly emotional and temporary. The commercial writer's techniques may seem arbitrarily chosen and employed piecemeal for momentary effects. The contexts are relatively free of implications. The reading experience ends neatly. The reader moves on to "consume" (as consumer of a product) the next story. A valid experience. One kind of experience.

There are many parallels between the writer and reader, between the art of writing and the art of reading. For the imaginative reader, rereading is a form of revision. W. H. Auden's statement "The innocent eye sees nothing" applies to both the writer and the reader. Both must learn, then know, what they are doing.

In the creative process, a writer moves from observation to inspiration to notes to conception to first draft, through revisions (from one to thirty), to a finished story. There are parallels between the writer's experience in writing the first draft and revising it and the reader's experience in reading the writer's finished story and re-reading it.

Flannery O'Connor was inspired somehow to write "A Good Man Is Hard to Find." There are many kinds of *inspiration*. Writers may write about a direct personal experience, focussing on themselves or someone who shared that experience (up to the killing, O'Connor, as a child, could have taken such a trip with her family). Writers base stories on experiences they have only observed (O'Connor could have watched such a family in a place like Red Sammy's). Writers may get some part of a story second hand, told to them by a person who experienced it or who witnessed or heard about it, or from the news media (O'Connor could have read a newspaper account of the escape and the killings). Inspiration for a story or a character or a concept may come to writers while they are reading other works of fiction or experiencing some other art form. Writers get ideas, sometimes full-blown stories, suddenly "out of nowhere," out of some subconscious eruption. Images or voices in dreams inspire some writers. Pure imagination is the source of many stories (O'Connor could have willfully conjured up this story from her imagination). Even a technique may inspire a story (O'Connor could have imagined the effect of opening a story with a conniving grandmother and closing it with a the cold-blooded killer of that grandmother).

We can imagine O'Connor asking herself, before the writing begins, "What do I want to do to the reader, and how do I do it?" and then, throughout all the revisions, asking *"Did* I do it? If not, *how* can I do it now?"

Reading over the first draft of "A Good Man Is Hard to Find," O'Connor may well have discovered, as many writers do, that she had been so superficial and literal-minded the reader had no way to become involved in the story.

O'Connor had to take her story through one or many more drafts, making revisions, each of which was intended to affect *you*, the reader, emotionally, imaginatively, and intellectually through all the story's facets with greater and greater immediacy, intensity, and lasting effect.

Just as you, whatever your level of understanding about fiction, struggle in your room to read "A Good Man Is Hard to Find," imagine the author struggling in her room to make a series of choices—effective or inept, ranging over every element of fiction—in various drafts.

In *A Writer's Diary*, Virginia Woolf describes her study as "that solitary room" where "life is subjected to a thousand disciplines and exercises . . . . Where I write variations on every sentence; compromises; bad shots; possibilities . . . ."

In the revision process, writers may *add* to or *cut* out a sentence, a paragraph, a scene. They may *substitute* one word, phrase, sentence, paragraph, passage for another. They may *reorganize* passages and scenes. They may shift or *recombine* material. They may make these changes to make the point of view more appropriate and consistent (or to change the point of view); to improve the style; to sharpen images; to repeat and relocate motifs; to create symbolic patterns; to develop characters more fully; to improve the use of various devices; to focus the structure more dramatically and meaningfully; to make the beginning or the ending more effective; to clarify the theme. Some writers revise even after publication, when a story is about to get reprinted. The last story O'Connor wrote was a total reconception of her first story.

For those students who feel "stupid" and irritated as they read a story because they know they are missing, page by page, what "the writer is trying to say," and who come out of class discussion feeling even worse, it may be some encouragement then to know that the story you are struggling with was written by a person who had to struggle page by page to understand, to see what he or she was creating. With each new story, the writer has to learn, in a sense, how to write *that* story, and so you have to learn how to read each new story.

Students, those who love to read as well as those who don't, ask, "Why study fiction; why not just read it?" One answer is that as you study fiction you develop an ability to respond more fully to every aspect of a story. The writer struggles through the revision process to create the story you are reading. The act of reading that story, whether it is easy or difficult, is also a part of the overall creative process.

Just as O'Connor could never have been fully aware of *all* the effects she had created, you may feel things in reading "A Good Man Is Hard to Find" that you can never quite describe or analyze. Just as earlier conscious study of their art enables writers to produce more and more effective first drafts of their stories, your conscious scrutiny of the way fiction works will enable you to respond more readily to a writer's many intentions the first time you read a story.

Perhaps before asking such questions as "What is the writer trying to say?" students and teachers might ask, "*What* did the writer *do* to me, and *how* did he or she do it?"

7

SOME DIFFERENCES BETWEEN THE USUAL WAY OF READING AND READING FOR STUDY

There are natural differences between the way you usually read and the way you read when you are a student who is trying to develop greater receptivity to all the elements at work in fiction. Students and instructors attempt to bring to conscious attention, for description and analysis and understanding, responses that are not typically conscious as we read. Readers who have studied the nature and effect of fiction may more fully respond to all the experiences the writer has imagined for the reader. When readers are receptive to literary fiction, they become collaborators, in a sense, with the writer in the creative process.

It is important to keep always in mind the fact that all readers *experience* a story first, before they come aware of the components of its quality: effectiveness of characterization, skillful development of conflict, brilliance of style. Even scholars, critics, and other serious readers, including writers, seldom subject a story to critical analysis during a first reading, and they never get around to giving many good stories a second reading.

Most stories are read in the normal course of daily life, as magazine stories are read, once, on the move. Originally, most of the stories in a text-anthology appeared in small-circulation literary publications (*The Yale Review, The Southern Review*) or in large-circulation commercial magazines (*The Atlantic, Redbook, Playboy, The New Yorker*), perishable, transient media of communication. Each magazine creates its own environment, which we approach with certain attitudes and enter with rather clear expectations, and in which we experience various effects, before, during, and after we read a story. Usually, we move on, leaving that issue of the magazine and its stories behind. A text-anthology is a different kind of environment. Each story affects the reader within an academic context—an atmosphere, usually, of a high seriousness that can be very stimulating in its own way.

Writers and readers would benefit mutually from a shared knowledge of a psychological study of the reading process and of the relation of that process to the creative process. Short of that, we can expect that an awareness of our own reading habits, of what happens to us in the act of reading fiction, will enhance our less conscious responses to the stories we read. For instance, how readily do you convert the words you are reading on the page into vibrant, coherent images in your mind? For some readers that conversion is difficult. An increased understanding of how fiction works may cause a decrease in that difficulty.

Writers are also readers and readers also write, if not fiction, then papers for classes, answers to exam questions, letters, diaries, etc. What is the common ground between writers and readers? Your own answers to such questions may enhance your responses to the written word.

Here are some *questions students often ask* (sometimes rather skeptically phrased); some may be your own:

How can a teacher say a *student's interpretation* of a story does not apply, when sometimes the author wasn't even sure of the meaning?

Do teachers create *symbols* that aren't there?

Should authors explain their *symbolism*? Do writers really think of all *the little "twists"* that English teachers find in a story?

What causes a writer's style to be the way it is?

Why do many writers use such *"flowery" language*?

In studying a story, why isn't more emphasis placed on *major points* instead of secondary details?

What details might be disregarded in studying a story?

How can you tell what the *tone* of a story is?

What is more important in a story, the structure or the *theme*?

Do writers *plan* their stories? When they begin, do they know
   how they will *end*, or do they decide while writing the
   story?

Is it more difficult to write an original draft or to *revise* a story?

Because serious fiction's finer qualities are not immediately
apparent, especially to the untrained sensibility, the study of fiction is necessary as a means of refining one's perceptions. The
techniques and emphases of serious writers are frequently not
the same as those of commercial writers. When they are similar,
the serious writer uses them in very different and more complex ways. The reader who has not yet learned to perceive these
differences in method may find some serious stories incomprehensible.

The study of a given story trains you to be more responsive
to stories you do not study. At first, some of the stories you read
in the text-anthologies may shock, frighten, confuse, or depress
you. But you may come to see that those stories have qualities
of beauty and delight that only a greater understanding and
appreciation of the nature and techniques of fiction can reveal.

Readers want the writer to learn to write well; the writer
expects readers to learn to read well. The purpose of this book
is to provide an understanding of techniques for interpreting
those experiences. Because interpretation requires work, it may
temporarily diminish some of the pleasure of reading fiction. But
the assumption is that gradually you will become convinced that
"tearing a story apart" is not a destructive act. Rather it is a
way of tracing the path of the creative process, a way of seeing,
feeling, and thinking about the whole, a way of enjoying the
thing itself by delighting in our understanding of how it works
and how it affects us. The "tearing apart" is simultaneously a
putting back together process.

The focus here is not only upon learning how to read each
work of fiction, but upon studying how that work *affects the
reader* in such a way that you learn how to read fiction of your
choice—whether commercial or literary—after the course ends.
Even as you are studying individual works for their own values,

you are learning about fiction in general. Studying each story for its own sake is less important than seeing how some aspect of the creative process is employed in it. So, whether you think a story is good or mediocre, whether it bores you or changes your life, is not the main issue. You can learn a great deal about technical aspects even from a story you continue to dislike.

It is extremely important as you move through this book to remember that critical analysis is a conscious, deliberate act of *secondary importance.* No teacher, no general reader can describe with subjective lyricism or delineate with critical analysis the most important aspects of the experience of reading a story, an act that is as individual as it is communal, just as writing is mysterious though also discussable. But a discussion of those secondary elements can develop a conscious or unconscious receptivity to everything a writer has consciously or unconsciously achieved. This point needs to be stressed: analyzing stories is never intended to be the same as, nor a substitute for, reading them in the more usual way. Analysis is a temporary means toward achieving a lasting ability. Once you have spent a reasonable amount of time consciously examining your responses to the artistry of these writers, you will be more responsive to all other fiction.

This reminder may help: writers rewrite to improve their stories; readers re-read to respond more fully to the experiences the story provides. In the first reading, as in the first writing, the focus is on experiencing the story and gaining an impression of the whole. A single reading provides one kind of experience; repeated readings extend that first experience as you discover more intricate relationships among all the elements in the story. Your experience of those elements becomes more complex, more pleasurable, more lasting. Re-examination, then, in no way diminishes your responses; it enhances them, emotionally, imaginatively, and intellectually.

This analytical process may modify your reading tastes; you may discover that some fiction that you now enjoy is less satisfying and that you will want to choose also from many other kinds of stories. Enjoyment, pleasure, entertainment—those words describe the reading of serious fiction just as aptly as they do commercial fiction, despite the differences between the two.

TWO
THE ART OF WRITING FICTION

1

THE ELEMENTS

The writer says, implicitly, to reach readers of each of his or her stories: "I want you to enjoy the development of these *characters* in this time and place *setting*, moving along this *story* line, engaged in this *conflict*, expressing this meaning or *theme*."

These are the constantly interacting elements that most readers are aware of as they read, inspiring such comments as: "Miss Brill is a pathetic character." "The southern landscape of 'A Good Man Is Hard to Find' was fascinating, and the story held my interest. I kept reading to find out what would happen next." "The conflict between the young black narrator in "Battle Royal" and his own classmates was worse than his conflict with the white leaders." "Invisible man is an excellent image for the theme of 'Battle Royal.'"

CHARACTER

Character is "the heart of fiction." Before you can become interested in the development and outcome of the conflict in a story, you must care about the main character, the *protagonist* (who struggles *for* something). In commercial stories, more often than in serious stories, the conflict is often more interesting than the characters because the emphasis is on what happens. The fact that the protagonist is a good person compared with the antagonist (who struggles *against* something) wins the reader's sympathy enough to compensate for any lack of characterization; our interest is fixed upon an external conflict between the main character and the enemy.

But in most serious stories the writer's interest is more in delineating character than in developing a story line. Katherine Mansfield wants us to become interested in her complex delineation of the character of Miss Brill in a very simple story—actually an episode. But that episode reflects everything about Miss Brill and her life, which consists of staying in her room or reading to an old man or, especially, walking in the park. Neither she nor the reader is even aware of an external conflict until the young couple make negative comments about Miss Brill, which destroys the major source of enjoyment in her life. That external conflict is a catalyst for the most important internal conflict between Miss Brill's perception of the life she observes and our awareness of the reality of it.

Miss Brill is interesting because of the way her imagination transforms reality to suit her psychological needs and attitudes; but Mansfield enables us to see simultaneously that every negative observation Miss Brill makes applies ironically to herself and that even her positive observations are all threatened by sudden reality. Although Mansfield does not develop story in the usual sense, she plots the development of the conflict between what Miss Brill imagines and brutal reality.

As you analyze a character and the nature of his or her conflict, bring the following considerations to bear:

1. Commercial writers employ oversimplified or *stock characters* to manipulate the reader's responses to the story; readers of commercial fiction may know that people are complex, but they prefer simple, familiar, predictable, comfortable characters. Stock characters are sometimes called *stereotypes*, or *flat* characters. With stock characters the writer can elicit *stock responses* from the reader: a grandmother in a rocking chair automatically gets a rather nostalgic or sentimental stock response from most readers.[1]

2. To make readers feel they have had an emotional experience, writers may employ one or more of a battery of tricks. They may merely *tell* about the grandmother's fine qualities instead of showing her in action (showing might reveal her lack of depth as a character); they may *editorialize*, by making persuasive authorial comment on her goodness; they may use a *heightened style*, by poetisizing about her in "purple prose" or

---

[1] Please bear in mind that throughout this book comments about commercial or popular fiction are descriptive, not judgmental. For instance, both serious and commercial writers use stock characters; they use them differently for different effects.

by overwriting a scene involving her; they may resort to *melo-drama* by having someone menace her; more commonly, they will *sentimentalize* her by eliciting from the reader an emotion in excess of the occasion (her gladiola dies, the reader weeps). Stock characters lend themselves effectively to the development of simple external conflicts.

3. *Complex*, or *round*, characters, being more life-like, lend themselves more readily to the delineation of internal conflicts (two aspects of a character in conflict with each other). You may have had about Miss Brill the same reactions described above regarding stereotypes. Miss Brill *is* a stereotypical solitary, elderly woman whose life is simple and whose pleasures are few and fragile. What makes her complex is that Mansfield adds to Miss Brill's stock characteristics the power of imagination. As with stock characters, we are told as well as shown certain things about Miss Brill. There is editorial comment, heightened style, a little melodrama, a good deal of sentimentality. But one of the things that makes a character complex is the *way* a writer presents that character. Notice then that it is not Mansfield the author, but Miss Brill the character who is sentimental, melodramatic, and who makes "editorial" observations, etc. The effect Mansfield wants to create for the reader is one of irony. The placing of a stock character, then, in some sort of complex context helps make that character complex.

4. *Round* (as opposed to *flat*) or *complex* (as opposed to simple) characters are of three general types: *typical* (a "typical old maid" some readers will call Miss Brill); *universal* (Miss Brill has problems like all people everywhere in all times, and her reliance on illusions to fend off reality is universal); or *individual* (to the extent that she transforms reality in her imagination, Miss Brill is somewhat different from other women who are like herself).

5. To show, by contrast, the various aspects of a complex character, writers sometimes use minor characters called *foils*. For instance, her imagined defense of the woman in the ermine

toque who is spurned by a man, suggests that Miss Brill identifies subconsciously with the woman.

6. If a reader is to feel that a character is "true to life" and if we are to care about that character, the character's usual behavior must be presented in a *consistent* fashion, or a particular character may be deliberately inconsistent. Presentation of character should be consistent with other elements in the story. The character's significant actions must be motivated. Consistency and motivation make a character *convincing*, plausible, believable. If you found Miss Brill convincing, you probably felt that Mansfield presented her behavior consistently from start to finish: here is how *this* woman would behave in this situation. What motivates Miss Brill to go routinely to the park? She is subconsciously fleeing her solitary room that is like a death cell.

7. In most stories, the main character must undergo some sort of *crisis* that brings about a real *change*, in fortune or in attitude. The crisis for Miss Brill is hearing the devastating comments of the young couple; the change in her attitude and thus in her behavior is that she can no longer see life as a romantic drama and so she will no longer go to the park. Mansfield maintains consistency of character while depicting a change, because Miss Brill's change is *in character*. It would be out of character for Miss Brill to return to the park.

8. *How* does a writer *present* complex characters? By showing them in a *situation* that brings out the various aspects of their character—how they feel and think about themselves and others, what they say, and how they act and react. More may be *implied* than explicitly stated. Miss Brill feels more than she thinks, and thinks about others more than herself; she says very little, and reacts more than she acts. The situation of leaving her room, walking in the park and returning to her room brings out all her characteristics. The author does not *tell* us about Miss Brill; she *shows* us. All we are meant to think about Miss Brill is *implied*: that she is afraid of death and old age, that she has no perspective on herself in relation to others, that she

sometimes turns people into things and things into people, that she is deluded.

To understand the *function* of each character in a story and thus to understand the story's purpose, you might ask the following questions (apply them to Miss Brill):

What are the character's dominant traits, values, drives?

Is the character likeable or unlikeable? Does it matter in *this* story?

What is the character's dilemma and what is the conflict he or she is engaged in? Is the conflict resolved positively or negatively for the character? Why?

Is the character changed? How? Why? Or why not?

Does the character learn anything from the way the conflict is resolved? If so, what?

SETTING

Setting, in the simplest sense, is the time and place in which the action of a work of fiction occurs. (Place is sometimes called "locale.") But setting can be far more complex. There may be specific time and place considerations within a general context of time and place. Consideration of the setting often includes the cultural dimension of a time and place. For example, the setting of "A Good Man Is Hard to Find" is the Deep South. More specifically, the setting is a house in Atlanta, then a car traveling over the Georgia landscape, a restaurant beside the highway, and finally a ditch in a remote rural area. The time is probably the early 1950's. And this story deals with cultural changes in America as seen in special ways in the South and as a contrast to timeless spiritual dilemmas.

Setting may, as in this story, produce conflict and be an expression of character: rural and urban Georgia produced this particular family and these particular three convicts. The basic elements of O'Connor's story could have been worked out in a great many other settings, but her use of the details of *this* setting enhances every moment in the story. The roadside restaurant provides a transitional setting between the neighborhood in Atlanta and the isolated ditch in the woods.

Several time and place settings may be only implied in a story. Notice how a sense of East Tennessee, the grandmother's native region, and the Federal Pen in Atlanta hover over the actual settings. And the historical past—the era when the grandmother grew up—hovers over the fleeting moments of the present. We see highways and country roads, shacks, graveyards, and the filling station-dance hall, called the Tower, while plantation mansions loom in the background.

The role of setting is always important, but more so in some stories than in others. The ballroom in the leading hotel in a small town in the South in "Battle Royal" is more symbolic of the larger setting of the South, with the cultural dimension of black-white relations, than are the shifting settings of "A Good Man Is Hard to Find." Both time and place are important in every story set in the South, or in New England or the West, or in New York City, or at sea. The metropolitan park as setting is important in "Miss Brill," but London is not; Central Park in New York in that era would have served almost as well. But Mansfield makes the most, in a very few pages, of *that* park in *that* city.

Readers find some settings more appealing than others; in fact, local color fiction, a type of writing that flourished from about 1880 to 1920 in America, placed more emphasis on regional setting than on character and story. If a writer dwells mostly upon a character's thoughts, time and place becomes a question of psychological processes, as in "Miss Brill." Specific place and chronological time are subordinate in that story.

As you read a story, determine what the time and place and the cultural settings are; on second reading ask yourself to what extent, and in what ways, the settings are important to the other elements in the story—character, conflict, plot, theme.

STORY AND PLOT

Of the three stories you have just read, "A Good Man Is Hard to Find" has more narrative or *story* elements than the other two, but not a more complicated *plot*. Although story and plot are often used synonymously, they are quite different.

Story derives from the Latin *historia*, history; it is a narrative composed of a sequence of events, incidents, or episodes. A family in Atlanta sets out in a car for a vacation in Florida; they eat at a roadside restaurant; the grandmother convinces her son to turn down a country road, seeking a plantation; they wreck; three escaped convicts kill them one by one and take their car. That is the story, the sequence of events O'Connor presents.

Plot, on the other hand, is the author's organization of all the story's elements, the joining of the events with the shape or structure of the narrative in such a way as to suggest the meaning: the mean-spirited members of a Southern middle-class family set out together in a car for a vacation in Florida; in the car and at lunch in a gaudy roadside restaurant they are constantly in dispute over trivial matters. The manipulative, pretentious grandmother cons them into turning off the main highway onto a dirt road in search of a plantation she recalls from her "superior" childhood. The car accidentally runs off into a ditch. Three escaped convicts kill them one by one, despite the grandmother's attempt to manipulate the leader, the Misfit, as she has manipulated the family. The Misfit declares "There's no real pleasure in life," but his dissatisfaction with life is far deeper than that of the members of the family he has slain.

For commercial fiction, a simple presentation of the story suffices; but in serious fiction the writer shapes or structures all the story's elements to express a concept or a meaning. O'Connor's *story* is interesting enough; her *plot* is far more interesting, complex, and ironic. The car wreck and the methodical executions are less important to O'Connor than what the people in that situation suggest about the quality of life, especially spiritual life. The grandmother is an ordinary person who mistakes good manners for ethics and superficial attitudes for religion. Except, ironically, on the superficial level of manners, the Misfit does not in any way fit into her world; his spiritual anguish is so profound it has turned him into a killer of such people as the grandmother. The wreck of the car is an important event only because it throws the family into a confrontation with the Misfit; the killings are important only as an expression of the grotesquely comic futility of living the kind of "good" life these average people think they are living. O'Connor deliberately undercuts the power of the story element—by defusing the potential for *suspense* and by her use of comic elements—to develop the form and meaning of a plot.

When you sense, usually early in a work of fiction, that the author is not going to emphasize story, as in "Miss Brill," try to accept that lack and look for other elements of interest, such as character analysis, and try to trace the development of the plot. Literary writers do not always tell stories, but they always *plot* their fiction. For instance, Mansfield almost never told stories, but in "Miss Brill," she plotted the movement of a woman from self-delusion to rude awakening.

CONFLICT

All effective fiction has conflict, but not necessarily the *external conflict* between a protagonist and an antagonist that most readers expect a *story* to deliver. Commercial fiction does not exclude internal conflict, but favors external. Suppose your friend asks, "What's it about?" "What happens in it?" If you replied, "It's about a young black man who tries to win some money in a free-for-all boxing event against several other young black men," your friend might well want to read it. Most people crave "a good tale." But if you told your friend, "It's about the life-long conflict within an anonymous young black man between his ambition to get ahead in a white man's world and his sense of guilt for not fighting for his own and his people's basic human rights," your friend might be less interested. If the first reply inspired your friend to start reading, his or her interest might bog down in the first few pages. If the second reply got a response, the inner conflict is so dramatically enacted in all the events in the ballroom, your friend could be all the more caught up in the story. The balance between the two kinds of conflict and the way, from moment to moment, they enhance each other is unusually effective in "Battle Royal."

In commercial fiction, there must be an external conflict; in serious fiction, even external conflicts often enhance the impact of an *internal conflict*. If you remove the internal conflict, "Battle Royal" makes no sense; if you remove the external conflict, the internal conflict becomes too abstract even for the most serious reader.

In "Battle Royal" the nature of the conflict on both levels, external and internal, finally takes us away from the focus on the main character to a consideration of the broad issues of race relations and even further to the universal problem each person has of feeling alienated from his supposed proper "place" in society. But *as we read*, that anonymous voice of the narrator keeps our attention so focussed on character that we feel both types of conflict and all the issues very keenly.

Here are a few questions about conflict to consider as you read the stories in this anthology ("Battle Royal" provides examples):

1. Who is most affected by events in the story? Who is the *protagonist*? Who is his or her *antagonist*? In "Battle Royal," obviously the anonymous narrator is the protagonist, but he is also his own antagonist in the conflict within himself. Ellison places all the other characters (his own grandfather, the white fathers of the community, his fellow classmates, the naked white woman) against him in the external conflict only to dramatize that inner conflict.

2. Are the protagonist and antagonist, the opposing forces, relatively *equal in strength*? Usually, they *should be* so that there can be *suspense* as to the outcome, the resolution. In "Battle Royal," the opposing forces on both external and internal levels—and the larger conflicts between blacks and whites, between the narrator's conflicting attitudes—are far stronger than the narrator, but he can, as here, win partial victories on both levels throughout his life.

3. What is the protagonist's *dilemma,* or *crisis situation?* Most of the conflicts in "Battle Royal" already exist before the story begins, but a distinct crisis situation is created when the narrator, as a young man, discovers he must fight in a battle royal before he is permitted to deliver the speech he expects will win the white leaders' approval.

4. Which kind of conflict is stressed, *external* or *internal?* To make that determination is important because your understanding of character depends upon it. When external conflict is stressed, character may be less important than action, or *story*; internal conflict always places the stress upon our interest in character. In external conflicts, the protagonist is trying, against opposition, to *accomplish* something. In the end, he wins or he loses. An internal conflict may pose a conflict between two sets of values. Ellison's narrator must *choose* between the values of humility and of revolt and act upon his decision. Is the conflict convincing and effective?

5. How *important* is the conflict to the protagonist and the antagonist, and to characters who align themselves with them? The outcome of the conflict must have a strong temporary or permanent effect on the character's behavior or values. The conflict and its outcome are very important to Ellison's narrator on both levels; it is unlikely that any other conflict could be more important or have a more profoundly lasting affect on him.

6. Is conflict the *main element* in the story, or is character analysis or meaning? Character and certainly meaning are ultimately important in "Battle Royal," but conflict is the immediate focus of our interest as we read. There may also be an implied surrounding conflict (as in "Battle Royal," where the historical black-white and Civil War conflicts intensify the personal conflict for the narrator) that intensifies our awareness of the main conflicts.

7. How does the author *organize* the conflict? Because external conflict depends upon a strong narrative thrust, the *chronological* presentation of events is usually most effective, leaving the outcome in *suspense,* with the resolution coming

at the end. When an inner conflict is being presented, the writer may reveal the resolution early and then tell how it came about, departing from chronology. *What* happens next is not as important as *why* the inner conflict exists and how it was resolved. In the first paragraph, Ellison's narrator tells us that he has been thinking about his inner conflict for twenty years.

8. Is the conflict clearly posed? Is it plausible? Is it *well-developed*? Do you feel a sense of necessity in the way one development follows another, step by step. Does the development of the conflict contribute, with *all* the story's other elements, to a unity of effect?

9. How is the conflict *resolved*? A story in which *only* an external conflict is developed will almost always result in the protagonist either winning or losing the contest with the antagonist. Ellison's narrator *wins* one external conflict—he gives his speech; but ironically, he *loses* the internal conflict, and so his win is *tainted* with dissatisfaction. In the long run, however, he continues to struggle within himself; that conflict remains *unresolved*. In this complex story, all four types of resolution are illustrated. Most stories contain only one of these.

The resolution must be plausible; it must reflect how people really behave. (Plausibility applies also to nonrealistic stories.) In "Battle Royal," the external conflict is resolved plausibly. But the inner conflict is so enormous and complex that it could not have been plausibly resolved.

10. What is the *function* of the conflict? To generate *narrative* or to reveal *character*? In "Battle Royal" the *focus* is on character.

11. If *sex* or *violence* figures in the conflict, is it there for its own sake or is the author's use of it justified? Commercial writers sometimes provide a little more sex or melodrama than the situation calls for to distract from inadequate character motivation or implausibility in the development of conflict. But Ellison's use of both sex and violence in "Battle Royal" are entirely justified as factors in both the internal and external conflicts. For instance, that the white men abuse women much as they abuse blacks

suggests something about the nature of impersonal sex and a lust for violence.

12. What *devices* does the writer use early in the story to suggest the conflict to come? Ellison, for instance, uses *foreshadowing*. The narrator's grandfather foreshadows the conflict. Commercial writers often plant information or an object to prepare for the presentation of a coincidence that mechanically resolves the conflict later on.

13. Is the ending *believable*? Does the writer contrive a happy ending to the conflict when we know the protagonist should, realistically, lose? Most readers dislike unhappy endings. Yet, few serious stories end happily because they are based on problems found in real life.

Does the writer offer a surprise ending? Commercial writers sometimes manipulate character and plot to produce a surprise ending. It becomes the sole reason for the story; knowing the ending, readers seldom reread a surprise-ending story. That device was perfected by O. Henry, but poorly imitated by many other writers. Such endings are seldom justified, but in some serious fiction—for example, William Faulkner's "A Rose for Emily" —a surprise ending suddenly illuminates all the complex elements leading up to it.

THEME

Out of conflict emerges some *generalization* about life, either topical or universal. That is what is meant by the term *theme* or *meaning*.

The first few pages of "Battle Royal" reveal the narrator's preoccupation, over twenty years, with making generalizations about his internal and external conflict experiences. The simple fact that he thinks of himself as anonymous and invisible indicates his primary interest in understanding the meaning of his experience, of race relations, and of the general human condition.

Sometimes the theme of a serious fiction is *topical*, or temporary, pertaining to one time, one place: the plight of one young black man in one small southern town in the 1930s. More often it is *universal*, or pertaining to all mankind, everywhere, always: the consequences, social and spiritual, of the black man's feeling that he is invisible, which is a metaphor for the human condition. By combining these two types in a single story, Ellison achieves greater impact and relevance.

You, like most readers, will have trouble sometimes grasping the theme of stories. The difficulty arises from the nature of serious fiction: writers do not *tell* you the meaning, they *imply* it by showing meaning as it is embodied in the elements of fiction—setting, story and plot, characters, conflict—and by presenting those elements through techniques—point of view, style, tone, symbols, allusions, etc. To come up with implied meanings, look at how all of a story's elements and techniques interact.

Here are some observations that may help ("Battle Royal" provides examples):

1. The theme or meaning of a story is not simply the subject. *Race relations* is the general subject of "Battle Royal," as it is for hundreds of different stories, but a statement of theme is more complex: the young black man's humble adaptation of the white man's image of blacks as a means of advancing in the white man's world ironically blinds him to contradictions and injustices so that he conspires in rendering himself invisible to others and to himself. That is *one* possible way of stating the theme of *this* race relations story.

2. *There is never one correct statement of the theme.* No reader can state the theme entirely as the writer intended, because each reader brings his or her own experiences to the story. My statement of the theme, given above, is neither entirely right, nor entirely wrong. But what makes it one viable statement among others is that it can be supported by almost every line in the story. If your statement of theme fails that test at numerous points, you need to question your interpretation. Without substantiation, an opinion is worth little.

Remember that the author's own statement may not pass the test as fully as one might expect. This paradox derives from the nature of fiction, which does not allow a scientifically precise answer to questions raised. That is its strength. Fiction enables us to experience and then think about human problems, not necessarily solve them, to raise questions, not answer them. Ten writers, telling Ellison's story, would generate ten different meanings. But no well-written story is open to free-for-all-interpretation. The important aspect of this paradox is that the writer and the readers can come quite close to consensus as to a basic statement of the theme. Build your individual interpretation upon common ground.

3.   The theme of a serious story cannot, like religious parables or commercial stories, be reduced to a moral, a lesson, or a maxim, such as: Playing the white man's game to advance yourself will often backfire. That is true of "Battle Royal," but as a statement of theme it is oversimplified and prevents a reader from seeing deeper, more complex, more wide-ranging issues. Serious writers and readers know there is an important difference between teaching a lesson and revealing an insight, between preaching about and interpreting life. Teaching and preaching often insist upon absolutes. Fiction reveals insights that are not *always* true; they are sometimes illuminating ambiguities.

4. You, like many readers, may have gotten the impression that the main reason for reading a story is to extract its meaning. Talk about meaning comes more easily and naturally in a classroom than talk about other elements or about the techniques of fiction. But it is important to remember that writers generally place no more importance upon meaning than they do upon other aspects of the nature and effects of fiction. Each element has its own important place and function, but its effect depends upon interaction with all other elements.

5. Other elements in fiction (and the style and technique of fiction) enable readers to enjoy a story even when they totally disagree with the author's meaning. O'Connor is one of America's most emphatically Christian writers; many Christians will find her vision disturbing but they, along with non-Christians, will enjoy "A Good Man Is Hard to Find" and her other stories for other reasons.

Commercial writers appeal to stock opinions and prejudices, to ideals embodied in mythic heroes, to what readers already believe, or yearn to believe; they know that readers insist on a theme as simple as a moral or message, as an excuse for enjoying other more exciting elements. Such themes merely label experience.

The serious writer's aim is to interpret experience. Although commercial writers inadvertly interpret our lives by employing mythic figures and events based on popular legends, serious writers assume that to some degree the reader's beliefs are always in flux. They may start with a stock theme in order to examine, expose, criticize, modify, or enrich it; they may present relatively new interpretations of experience, or at least original perspectives on old ideas. They may suggest fresh ways of looking at specific human problems or offer new general visions of life. Again, the main purpose of commercial fiction is to entertain within familiar contexts. The main purpose of serious fiction is to entertain while presenting fresh interpretations of experience.

2
The Techniques

What *conception* of human experience is the author developing in the story? To answer that question, you need to know how the writer employs various techniques to orchestrate the interaction of all the elements of fiction: character, setting, story and plot, conflict, and theme. A study of the writer's techniques develops your receptivity to the effects of those techniques—what they *do* to you the reader and *how* they do it.

A technique may be defined as any method a writer uses, consciously or unconsciously, to stimulate an emotional, intellectual, or imaginative response in you, the reader.

The writer strives for such a unity of all the elements that the story becomes like a living organism. "Cut a good story anywhere," said Chekhov, "and it will bleed." Not a single word of "Miss Brill," for example, can be cut without wounding the entire organism.

The two techniques that all writers use are *point of view* and *style.*

NARRATIVE POINT OF VIEW

All their lives, writers struggle with narrative point of view; it is the most difficult technique to master. It is no surprise then that readers discover that discussing and writing about point of view are confusing and frustrating.

But if you consider the fact that in your everyday life you use the same three primary types of narrative that writers use, perhaps that will make the workings of the point-of-view technique clearer.

Almost every day, you tell stories to people—about yourself or about other people. "I ran a red light this morning, and . . . ." In fiction, that's called *first person* narration. The author lets one character tell the story: "There was still laughter as I faced them, my mouth dry" ("Battle Royal").

You *empathize,* almost every day, with other individuals—you put yourself in their shoes. Your mother fears growing older and you imagine how she feels. That's called *central intelligence* narration. The author filters (centralizes) everything that happens in the story through the mind of one character, using the third person: "Miss Brill felt a tingling in her hands and arms, but that came from walking, she supposed."

And you take a general view, or overview, nearly every day, of some aspect of your life. You ran a red light this morning, your mother fears growing older, you suspect you are overdrawn at the bank, and you are unprepared for the chemistry final tomorrow. Life is hard. That summary view is similar to *omniscient* narration in fiction. The author narrates, giving an overview of what's happening: "They turned onto the dirt road . . . . The children were thrown to the floor and their mother, clutching the baby, was thrown out the door onto the ground; the old lady was thrown into the front seat. The car turned over . . . " ("A Good Man Is Hard to Find").

In each of the above three instances, you are the authority for what you tell about the stop sign incident, for how you empathize with your mother, for the generalizations about your life. In each of the three types of fictive narration, the writer creates a particular kind of voice that is the source of authority for everything presented in each story. You, the reader, respond to that voice.

To illustrate to yourself how these three types of narrative points of view differ, rewrite (in your head or on paper) the openings of each of the three stories:

"A Good Man Is Hard to Find": Let the grandmother start the story in the first person. Next, start the story inside Bailey's mind in the third person.

"Battle Royal": Start the story as if you were an omniscient narrator. Next, start it as if you were inside the narrator's head.

"Miss Brill": Let Miss Brill tell her own story in the first person. Next, become an all-knowing (omniscient) narrator and describe Miss Brill entering the park.

We may imagine writers similarly considering possible point-of-view techniques—O'Connor, for instance, asking herself, "Should I let the grandmother, or Bailey, or the mother, or one of the kids, or the Misfit tell the story in the first person? No, I don't want the reader to be inside any of these characters, looking out, listening; I want the reader to see them all, to watch them. Besides, how could any member of the family tell the story? They all die in the end. The Misfit knows only what happens *after* the wreck. I want the reader to live with this family, with a focus on the grandmother, *before* the Misfit encounters them. How about the central intelligence point of view? Should I present everything through the perceptions of the grandmother, some other member of the family, or the Misfit? No, that would limit me too much. The experience I want to subject the reader to requires that I have free access to all the characters. So I will use the omniscient point of view, still focussing on the grandmother."

When we use the term "point of view" in everyday life, we use it in the sense in which it is used in this example: "I respect your point of view." But in this text, "point of view" is used in *this* sense only: "In 'Battle Royal,' the point of view technique Ralph Ellison uses is first person." Point of view in fiction is a technique the author uses, *not* an opinion a person holds. Nor does "point of view" refer, in this text, to a *character's* position in time and space in relation to other characters, as in this statement: "The narrator's point of view on the people and events in the story is that of an observer, not a participant." To insure clarity, please keep these distinctions in mind.

OMNISCIENT
The author tells the story

In the omniscient point of view, authors narrate the story in the third person, although they *may* speak now and then in first person, as Dickens and Thackeray do. The omniscient narrator is godlike, seeing, hearing, feeling, knowing all, moving anywhere in time and space, shifting from one character to another, giving the reader objective views of the characters' actions or subjective views of their thoughts. The roving, omniscient narrator strives for a balance between interior and exterior views of the characters.

No specific omniscient narration illustrates *all* the characteristics described above.

To return to every day experience as a parallel, suppose you read in the newspaper an account of the massacre of a family. Suppose the killers were not known, but that you had read earlier that the Misfit and his two fellow convicts had escaped. You would rather easily and naturally put together a somewhat omniscient view of those two factual events, and your imagination would add, without much effort, several elements. Your own overview would stimulate your emotions, your imagination, your intellect. Something along those lines *may* have been the case with O'Connor.

Suppose you then meet a friend who has not read about the events and you tell him what happened. "I'll bet it was the Misfit and his men who shot those people," you might say. Then you might begin to tell *your* version of what happened, narrowing your focus, probably to the Misfit, because the news accounts focus on him. But a writer imagines many more possibilities and takes a deeper interest in all of the people involved. O'Connor settles upon the grandmother, while moving now and then into a general view: "*They* all sat down at a board table . . . ." You have often, then, engaged in an activity quite similar to that of an omniscient narrator; the difference is that the fiction writer *controls* all the elements to have certain effects upon a reader such as yourself.

Usually the author will signal the reader early that the point of view is omniscient. The first line is "The grandmother didn't want to go to Florida." Then later, "Bailey was the son she lived with, her only boy." This is the kind of background information an omniscient narrator gives readers; the grandmother herself would not think in those terms at that moment. Up to the passage in which "they" enter the cafe, the focus on the grandmother reads almost as if the point of view were central intelligence. But "He and the grandmother discussed better times" puts the emphasis momentarily on Red Sam. "She discussed better times with Red Sam" would be the way a central intelligence narrator would phrase that line. "They saw a car . . . coming slowly as if the occupants were watching them" is the author's point of view. "The grandmother stood up and waved both arms dramatically to attract their attention" is the author juxtaposing a menacing image to an action that shows the grandmother's ironic lack of awareness. You can see that the effect at this moment would be very different had the author placed you inside the grandmother's mind *only* (central intelligence) at this moment, in this context.

After the grandmother is killed, O'Connor shifts to a sharp focus on the Misfit. That would not have been effective had O'Connor started and stayed inside the grandmother's mind only, using the central intelligence point of view. The importance of point of view as a technique that determines what and how the reader experiences elements in a story is suggested by this question: What would we as readers have lost had O'Connor made the grandmother the central consciousness instead of employing omniscience, especially in those last fifteen lines? In this case, the question is truly debatable.

Each type of point-of-view technique allows the writer particular freedoms and imposes particular limitations. The omniscient narrator is the freest, but the author's freedom may lead to excess, lack of focus, loss of control. The reader may feel that the omniscient narrator, who sees and knows all and can go anywhere, *ought* to tell all, should not withhold information, should not fail to render a scene that the reader knows can be rendered. But the omniscient narrator does not really have the total knowledge of a god; the writer knows that the reader knows that everything cannot, after all, be told.

The omniscient narrator may manipulate the reader intellectually or emotionally by intruding to make explicit authorial comments—to analyze, to philosophize, to render judgments on characters. The narrator may tell about characters in generalized commentary or summary narrative passages, or show them in dramatic scenes. Modern writers, critics, and readers generally object to commentary directly from the author because it shatters the illusion that real people are involved in real events. The emphasis today is on dramatic narration, conveying a sense of events happening now, not told as having happened in the past. Unity may be shattered also when a reader must reorient with each shift from dramatic scene to summary narrative to authorial commentary.

To solve the problems of classic omniscient narration, and to achieve dramatic immediacy, some modern writers create an *objective narrator*. The author is invisible; the author's voice is silent or neutral. As much as is humanly possible, the narrator avoids taking sides with one character against another, but is impartial, impersonal, disinterested. He or she refrains from expressing attitudes about controversies or social issues. Readers feel as if there is no narrator, as if they are watching a play, or a movie. This camera-eye objectivity can never be total, of course; words have too many uncontrollable connotations. Ernest Hemingway's "The Killers" is a good example of objective narration.

FIRST PERSON
A character tells the story

Traditionally, the author either narrated the story directly to the reader or allowed one of the characters to tell or write it. In a way, the first-person narrator has as much mobility and freedom and as much license to comment on the action as the omniscient narrator. Look closely at the first three paragraphs of "Battle Royal". Substitute "he" for "I" and those passages will sound like an omniscient narrator. But if the omniscient narrator's freedom is limited in some ways, the first-person narrator is even more limited. The first-person narrator cannot get into the minds of other characters as the omniscient, godlike, all-knowing narrator can; first-person narration is limited to those things the character has seen, heard, felt, or been told by other witnesses. But the advantage of first-person narration is that it is dramatically immediate, as all quoted speech is, and thus has great authority.

By allowing one of the characters to narrate the story, authors surrender partial control over the fictive elements. They must achieve their own purposes, which may be very different from those of their characters, through implication, irony, and other devices. For instance, Ellison is outraged by the way whites treat blacks, but his anonymous narrator very seldom directly criticizes his tormentors. How can the author convey his own attitude to the reader?

In this instance, as in all others, the reader must remember that the first-person narrator is *not* the author. Interpretation becomes muddled when readers forget, for instance, that Ellison is not the "I" speaking in "Battle Royal." The character-narrator is expressing his own subjective feelings and thoughts.

First person narration is perhaps the most favored technique today. To show how the three point of view techniques differ in their effect on the reader, look first at the passages on page 19 in which the narrator enters the hotel ballroom. The narrator is told that he is expected to participate in a battle royal with his classmates before he gives his speech to an all male audience gathered to have fun "on the occasion of a smoker." The context Ellison has created provides an implied irony: the classmates to whom the narrator gave his idealistic graduation speech about Negro-white relationships the day before he must now fight to entertain white men. There is an implied bitterness in the line "The battle royal came first," because we are aware that the narrator is writing about this event twenty years later, looking back, reflecting on the meaning of it all. It is in that spirit in that time frame that the reader experiences that passage and the rest of the narrative.

Suppose Ellison had started to write this story in his own voice as author (omniscient point of view); the opening might have sounded this way:

> On the occassion of a smoker, the town's leading white citizens had gathered in the main ballroom of the finest hotel to watch a naked white woman in a lewd dance and a bunch of black boys fight in a battle royal. One of these black boys had come to deliver an idealist speech on relations between blacks and whites. He was a little surprised to learn that the town fathers expected him to participate in a battle royal with the very classmates to whom he had delivered the speech at graduation the night before. It was not until some years later that the full irony of the situation would strike him.

In this omniscient point of view, the reader participates not with a character but with an author in a full awareness of the entire situation.

Now suppose that Ellison found that the omniscient style and tone put the reader at too great a distance from the character, causing him to turn to the central intelligence method:

> The excitement of being inside the town's leading hotel was accelerated as he stepped into the main ballroom. He saw that it was filled with the town's leading male white citizens. He sensed an absence of the aura of dignity he had imagined. When the mayor told him that before he could deliver to these gentlemen tonight the speech he had delivered to his classmates at graduation yesterday, there would be a battle royal among his own classmates, he was disoriented. "Since you're going to be here anyway, you may as well fight in it, too."

Readers experience everything in that passage as if they were the protagonist: the nervous excitement of being a young black man in the fine hotel as a special guest of the leading white citizens and the disorientation of being thrust unexpectedly into the lowest role a young black man can play— violent entertainer of overfed, drunken white community leaders.

But Ellison's purpose is to put his protagonist and his reader at a distance in time and space from that event, to enable both to reflect on the general situation *while* experiencing it. To achieve *that* purpose, the man's own first person narration, twenty years later, is more effective, than the omniscient or the central intelligence point of view would be.

The first person narrator combines the subjective (how he feels about what he sees) with the objective (he wants to *show* the reader). He is both omniscient storyteller and subject of his story. Perception is an act of self-discovery for him.

Some Questions to Ask When Reading First-Person Narrations

After you have read a first-person story, you may respond more fully to all its elements if you are able to answer some of the following questions. In some stories, answers may be stated or they may be only implied; many other stories may not, for various reasons, provide answers to all these questions, and that very lack of answers may provide part of the experience the writer wants you to have. Not all these questions apply to *every* story. As an example, apply these questions to "Battle Royal."

1. Is the narrator *speaking* or *writing?*
2. If the narrator is speaking, *to whom* is he or she speaking? To himself or herself? To one or more listeners? In dramatic monologue? (or duologue)? *How?* Stream of consciousness? Revery? Interior monologue? (Described below.)
3. If the narrator is *writing,* to *whom* is he or she writing? To himself or herself? *How?* diary? journal? report? To others? How many others? *How?* letter? confession? general publication, as in an autobiography or memoir?

Note: If it is not clear whether the narrator is speaking or writing, the author may rely on *literary convention,* that is, on the understanding between writer and reader that the writer need not, for certain effects, reveal whether the narrator is speaking or writing. It is *literary convention* to accept that.

4. *When* is the narrator speaking or writing (the time distance between the events being narrated and the actual narration of those events)?
5. *Where* is the narrator speaking or writing (the spatial distance between the locale of events being narrated and the place in which the narrator is speaking or writing)?
6. *Why* is the narrator speaking or writing to listeners or readers?

7. *Who* is the *surface focus* of the narrator's story? Me, him or her, them or us?
8. *Who* is the *submerged focus* (conveyed mostly by implication) of the narrator's story? Me, or him or her; them or us?
9. Is the narrator *reliable,* or *unreliable,* and to what degree?
10. What is the *effect* (in general and specifically, line by line) *on style* of the answer to each of these questions?
11. What is the *effect* (in general and specifically, line by line) *on the reader?*

First-person narrators may be major participants, minor participants, or witnesses to the stories they tell; or they may simply retell stories they have heard. In effect, they are saying, "This happened to me," or "This happened mainly to someone else." Each of these possibilities affects the story and thus the reader in different ways. They are not incidental, arbitrary elements; they are vital.

The *stream-of-consciousness* (thoughts and images flowing through a character's mind) and the *interior-monologue* (the character talks to himself in his mind) techniques provide the deepest, most intimate view of a character's feelings and thoughts. Stories employing these techniques exclusively are rare. The stream-of-consciousness technique offers a mingling of the character's conscious and involuntary thoughts. In interior monologues characters more consciously talk to themselves, silently. The *dramatic monologue* is the opposite: the character speaks directly to another character. Often a writer will intersperse objective narration at various points in an interior monologue, for contrast, sometimes with ironic intent.

CENTRAL INTELLIGENCE
The author filters the story through the conciousness of a character

In both the first-person point-of-view technique and the third-person, central-intelligence point-of-view technique, authors remove themselves from the story and work from inside the character outward. In central-intelligence narration, sometimes called limited omniscience, the story is presented in the third person, all the elements of the story are filtered through the perceptions and consciousness of a single character (the central intelligence), revealing his or her personality.

Turn now to the opening passage of "Miss Brill" on page 32. Notice that Mansfield presents to you only what Miss Brill sees ("blue sky powdered with gold"); tastes (implied: "white wine"); feels ("Miss Brill was glad," but she feels "a faint chill"); touches ("touched her fur"); smells (implied: "moth-powder"); thinks ("Dear little thing!"); hears ("the band"); knows ("the band played all the year round"). Miss Brill does not tell us about events in the park as the first person narrator would; she reflects them ("The band sounded louder" is Miss Brill's perception).

Usually, the author adjusts the style and vocabulary to the age, mentality, and social situation of the point-of-view character. Miss Brill is around fifty; she is imaginative and sentimental; and she is a teacher. It is as if the author were paraphrasing in the third person what the character would say if she were telling the story in the first person. "Little rogue! Yes, I really felt like that about it. Little rogue . . . ." is the way Miss Brill might have told the story herself. (But to whom? Her inability to talk directly to people is a large part of her problem.)

Many writers today favor the third-person, central-intelligence point of view. Its great advantage is that the reader consistently experiences everything through the character's own emotions, imagination, and intellect with intimacy and intensity. The limitation of this method is that it is a little weak dramatically, because the author cannot directly describe the character in action; he or she often remains physically passive, almost invisible.

The focus may be primarily upon the narrative experiences of the point-of-view character or upon his or her responses to the active experiences of a more dramatic character. The particular focus determines the reader's responses to the elements being developed in the story.

Just as readers sometimes mistakenly attribute to authors the attitudes of their first-person narrator, readers often forget that in central-intelligence narration, every perception is to be attributed to the point-of-view character. For instance, the rather precious, sentimental phrases and exclamations ("Oh, how sweet it was . . . !") in the first paragraph of "Miss Brill" are to be attributed not to Mansfield herself but to Miss Brill. As in the first-person narration, the immediate authority for everything in the story is the character (although the author is, of course, the ultimate authority). Because nothing goes into the story that the point-of-view character has not experienced, the author is more likely to include only what is truly relevant.

Because a character's perceptions may be limited, the writer must be very adroit in the use of such devices as implication, irony, and symbolism as ways of communicating to the reader more than the character can perceive. Miss Brill's perceptions are limited by her willful exclusion of reality, her insistence upon making life conform to her fantasies. The symbolism of the fur's box as a coffin (introduced in the first paragraph only as a box), the irony of Miss Brill's conviction that "No doubt somebody would have noticed if she hadn't been there" (the way the young couple do notice her crushes her), and the implication that she will never return to the park (perhaps never leave her room)—all that is presented indirectly by Mansfield to you the reader even as you empathize with Miss Brill.

* * *

The omniscient point of view was most appropriate and effective in times when the author might pretend to know all, to be the creator of the world he described, as Dickens could. Today's writers, feeling that to pretend to know all is an impertinence in a world so complex, specialize in selected areas of human experience, and use the mind of a single character through which to reveal those selected areas to the reader. However, some modern fabulists have returned to the omniscient point-of-view technique.

If writers use poor judgment in their choice of the point of view through which the elements of the story are presented, or if they mishandle the one they choose, they set up a chain reaction that demolishes most of their carefully prepared effects.

A story told in the third person will differ radically—in style, structure, and content—from the same story told in the first person. Readers may commit fallacies of interpretation if they fail to identify and follow the workings and implications of the point-of-view technique the author employs. The critical reader must feel that the point of view is the inevitable one for a given story.

Because it most directly affects the choice and use of all elements, point of view is the most important technique. In the creative process, a writer may ask: What is the best, the inevitable point of view for the effects I want to have on the reader? How does that point of view determine what the reader sees and feels? What does the point of view I have chosen express, in itself, about the story? How does this choice affect style, characterization, conflict, theme, structure? What is the psychological effect of presenting this story through the mind of the main character in the third person as opposed to letting the character tell it in his or her own voice? What are other possible points of view for this story and what are their particular effects? The student of fiction may ask similar questions about the published story.

As you reread a story, ask: How are conflict, characterization, and theme handled differently in the three different point-of-view techniques? What are some differences in style? in the use of other devices and techniques? in emotional effect? Of each story ask: What would happen to its elements and effects if it were told from each of the other two points of view?

Any of these three types of narrators may be active agents in the story's events, or physically passive but emotionally and intellectually active observers. The authority of each type of narrator as the source of all that happens in a story is affected by some degree of time and space distance. How close is the narrator's position in time and place to the characters and events?

Once readers identify the source of authority in a story, they must be careful not to accept that authority too literally or too fully. In the omniscient point of view, the author is usually a reliable authority for what the reader is told. But human perception is limited and faulty; therefore, what the first-person narrator tells or writes or what the central-intelligence character experiences should be carefully evaluated by the reader. For instance, in "Battle Royal" readers may tend to accept the narrator's attitude about people and his perception of events, but if they step back a little, they may perceive that the narrator is to some extent deceiving himself. And consider Miss Brill. She does not fully comprehend the implications of what she perceives and thinks, and Mansfield depends, for the story's full effect, upon the reader's ability to perceive and evaluate some things in ways Miss Brill, with her limited, faulty perception, cannot. In such stories, the essence of the reader's experience lies in the differences between the way the reader perceives the story's elements and the way the point-of-view character perceives them. The reader has, in a sense, a certain omniscience.

The effective use of point of view makes a greater demand on the writer's skills than any other technique. Every element in a story—character, setting, plot, conflict, theme—and every technique is controlled by the way the writer handles the point of view chosen. For instance, the author controls what the first person narrator says and how he says it in such a way that as he tells us about other characters, he reveals himself (as in "Battle Royal"). In central intelligence, the main character's perceptions reveal other characters to herself (as in "Miss Brill"). In first person and central intelligence, style creates the protagonists, and the other characters are revealed through them to the reader. In the omniscient point of view, the author focuses on one or two (or more) characters and creates constellations of characters around them (as in "A Good Man Is Hard to Find"). The author's style directly creates the main characters and the minor characters that surround them.

Writers strive to make the point of view consistent as one means of controlling all the elements of their stories. For instance, in the omniscient, writers avoid jumping from one character's mind to another's without careful transition or without reorienting the reader. In the first person, writers do not allow narrators to use a vocabulary they are not likely to have. In the third person, central intelligence, writers take care not to violate the point of view by attributing to characters things they couldn't know, think, or feel. Writers do not want their readers to become confused about whose evaluation of events they are getting.

Some writers use two or more *point-of-view techniques in combination.* For instance, one or more characters may tell parts of the story in the first person within a third-person-omniscient frame. Some writers juxtapose the third-person, central-intelligence points of view of two very different characters. In "Just Like a Tree," Ernest Gaines juxtaposes ten first-person narrators.

STYLE: The Author's Use of Words

The writer's medium is words. Despite its primary importance, *style* is one of the least discussed aspects of technique because it is difficult to describe its effects.

What, then, is style? Style is, narrowly speaking, the author's use of language: it is diction (intuitive or conscious choice of words), syntax (arrangement of phrases), and the handling of sentence and paragraph units by varying patterns; it is the use of figurative language (simile, metaphor). And more. Our responses to a story are controlled by language artfully arranged to achieve carefully prepared effects.

In a larger sense, style is a writer's own distinctive manner of expression. Few writers achieve a distinctive style of their own; it is easier to recognize most writers by their handling of techniques. But it is distinctive style that distinguishes most great writers from each other, Hemingway from Ellison, Faulkner from O'Connor, Fitzgerald from Mansfield.

To detect ways in which writers try to affect the reader, analyze their styles. The words writers choose to express feelings, thoughts, and actions will tell you a great deal about their relationship to the elements of their stories and the way they want readers to respond to them.

Is the style appropriate to the subject matter and to the point of view the author uses? Style and point of view are the major technical considerations in analyzing a story. Variations on the writer's basic style are somewhat determined by the particular point-of-view technique he or she decides to employ in a given story.

Style derives from that point-of-view technique. To show how point of view affects style, imagine O'Connor writing the opening paragraph of her omniscient story "A Good Man Is Hard to Find" from the two *other* point of view techniques: first person and central intelligence. Notice that when the point of view changes, the style, the author's choice of words, changes.

First Person (the grandmother narrating):

> I didn't want to go to Florida, I wanted to visit my connections in East Tennessee. Living with Bailey I didn't always feel appreciated. Bailey had hid himself behind the sports, but I didn't need to see his face to state my case. "Now look here," Bailey says, "see here, read this," and I rattle the front page at his orange sports page. "Here this fellow that calls himself The Misfit is aloose from the Federal Pen not two miles from where you sit so unconcerned and he's headed toward Florida and you read here what it says he did to these people. Just you read it. I wouldn't take my children in any direction with a criminal like that aloose in it. I wouldn't when *you* was a baby, because I couldn't answer to my conscience if I did." This time I am sure he will see it my way.

Central Intelligence (through the grandmother's perceptions):

> She didn't want to go with Bailey and the children and their mother to Florida, among the palm trees and the ocean waves; she wanted to show them the mountains and East Tennessee and her relatives there. She shook the front page over Bailey's head to distract him from his orange sports page, certain she could change his mind this time. "Now look here, Bailey, see here, read this," she said, standing with one hand on her hip.

Now re-read the first paragraph as O'Connor wrote it, page 2.

Notice that the *tone* is slightly different in each of the three versions. Rhythm and word choice account in part for those differences. Certain words that function effectively in one version are not effective in another. The phrasing in the central intelligence point of view suggests the rhythm of mental processes. In this context, the grandmother would neither think of nor speak of the fact that "Bailey was the son she lived with, her only boy," nor of her "thin hip," but an omniscient author would. "Connections" belongs in her vocabulary but somehow doesn't ring true in the other two versions. She wouldn't refer to Bailey's "bald head," nor describe in detail the way he sits at the table nor offer full information about the newspaper. The phrase *"rattling* the newspaper" works in all three versions. In the first person example, the use of "I" instead of "she" affects the tone. The linking of several sentences with commas conveys the rhythm of oral storytelling.

The style of most omniscient narrators is complex: a wide vocabulary range, compound sentences, long paragraphs. But the style of some omniscient authors has its own characteristics. O'Connor is known for mixing a complex style ("'But nobody's killed,' June Star said with disappointment as their grandmother limped out of the car, her hat still pinned to her head but the broken front brim standing up at a jaunty angle and the violet spray hanging off the side") with the tone and simple diction of her main characters ("This story tickled John Wesley's funny bone and he giggled and giggled but June Star didn't think it was any good").

If the omniscient point of view allows writers freedom of style it can also lure them into excess. Because omniscient narrators must be somewhat godlike, authors often feel the style must be elevated, so that it sounds like the voice of a godlike creator. The dangers of a complex, grand, or high style is that the author strains sometimes too hard to achieve eloquence, wit, lyricism, or memorable phrases, and bogs down in overstatement, overwriting. The complex style sometimes becomes pretentious, affected—overloaded with adjectives, ornamental metaphors, exotic phrases, archaic words, and formal phrases—making reading unneccessarily difficult for some readers.

In a first-person story, how appropriate is the style in relation to the character telling the story? Limited to that character's way of talking or writing, how does the author manage effects behind that limitation? The first paragraph of Ellison's "Battle Royal" is designed to do the work of a chapter in a novel: totally involve the reader, not with plot complications but with rhetorical intricacies submerged in a relatively plain style. "I was looking for myself and asking everyone except myself questions which I, and only I, could answer." That sentence alone, within the context of time set up by "It goes a long way back," suggests all the elements of a fiction that would need the scope of a novel to develop. And indeed, "Battle Royal," though a short story complete in itself, is incorporated into the early pages of Ellison's famous novel *Invisible Man.* The last line is a dramatically effective reversal of narrative sequence, sending us back to the beginning: "But first I had to discover that I am an invisible man!"

The narrator's style is perfectly suited to an educated man who is trying to simplify the complexities of his life. Since his story is one of self-discovery he does not explain to us what he now knows; he tells what he did and thought at a time when he had very little self-awareness or awareness of his surroundings. *Context* and *implication* are Ellison's techniques for giving his style a more complex effect. For instance, neither Ellison nor the narrator want to tell us directly that there is a parallel between the blond female dancer and the black male fighters; they imply it by applying the phrase "like drunken dancers" to the fighters.

An interviewer once asked Ellison why he shifted in the novel from one style to another–from realistic or naturalistic, to expressionistic, then to surrealistic. "In the South," Ellison replied, where his narrator "was trying to fit into a traditional pattern and where his sense of certainty had not yet been challenged, I felt a more naturalistic treatment was adequate." With each reversal in the narrator's fortune, Ellison shifted, in the novel, to a different, appropriate style. One can see in "Battle Royal," within the naturalistic style, stylistic foreshadowings of those shifts to other styles. For example, impressionism: "The room went red as I fell. It was a dream fall, my body languid and fastidious as to where to land . . . ." and expressionism: "Suddenly I saw a boy lifted into the air, glistening with sweat like a circus seal, and dropped, his wet back landing flush upon the charged rug, heard him yell and saw him literally dance upon his back, his elbows beating a frenzied tattoo upon the floor, his muscles twitching like the flesh of a horse stung by many flies."

Mansfield's style is perhaps more characteristic of that which most writers today employ. The style of most fiction is a careful amalgam of words that *denote* and words that *connote*; some writers use denotative words more than others; some strive for connotative effects and thus move closer to poetry. Some are too suggestive; some are not suggestive enough. Realistic writers choose details to create the illusion of actuality; impressionistic writers choose a different sort of detail for a different effect. But, like Mansfield, most writers try to evoke a sense of life rather than attempt to render it literally and totally. In fiction, language more often connotes than denotes. Mansfield's style usually works by *indirection*, even when she seems to be making a literal statement; she underwrites her most important scenes, understates her major insights.

The central-intelligence point of view Mansfield uses in "Miss Brill" restricts the style to the nature of the protagonist through whose eyes we see the story. In the opening paragraph of "Miss Brill," the words "brilliant" "fine," "gold," "light," and "glad" are rather denotative, in the context, but the words "chill," "iced water," "leaf came drifting," and "nowhere" connote a contrasting feeling of something negative about to happen. Mansfield tries to simulate Miss Brill's own thought processes with a style that is as informal as Miss Brill's own vocabulary: "And he'd been so patient. He'd suggested everything . . . ." To give an impression of Miss Brill's hyper-poetic sensibility, Mansfield offers lines like this: "Behind the rotunda the slender trees with yellow leaves down drooping, and through them just a line of sea, and beyond the blue sky with gold-veined clouds." "Down drooping" is a particularly "poetic" phrase.

"In 'Miss Brill,'" wrote Mansfield, "I chose not only the length of every sentence, but even the sound of every paragraph to fit her, and to fit her on that day, at that very moment."

Even cliché expressions can be controlled to create transcendent effects, as in "Miss Brill." "It was like a play" is a clichéd way of describing a scene in life that one finds pleasing and interesting. "It was exactly like a play." The word "exactly" puts an emphasis on Miss Brill's cliché that suggests compulsiveness. "Who could believe the sky at the back wasn't painted?" Now the "play" simile begins to get transformed into something that transcends the woodenness of the cliché expression. In the rest of that long paragraph, Mansfield develops the major metaphor of the story. Miss Brill's thrilling discovery will backfire on her today.

All fiction styles have certain elements in common. A few of those elements are *figurative language, repetition, denotation and connotation, concreteness versus abstraction, pace,* and *tension.* Some writers thrive on *metaphorical language* as do O'Connor ("her big black valise that looked like the head of a hippopotamus"), Ellison ("I am an invisible man!") and Mansfield ("the conductor . . . scraped his foot and flapped his arms like a rooster about to crow . . . "). But others carefully avoid it. In revision, Hemingway cut many metaphors. Writers quite naturally see comparisons all around them; each thing is like many other things. The problem is to include only those figures of speech that relate to and enhance a master design, as Ellison and Mansfield do particularly well; O'Connor's hippo image has only a momentary effect.

Prose, like poetry, has rhythm, cadence, and *texture,* and texture can act upon a reader's mind almost sensually. Perhaps you *felt* the tightly woven texture of Ellison's style, the loose texture of O'Connor style, the conversational, idiomatic texture of Mansfield's style. And texture will affect a reader's attitude toward what is read. Some reader's will resist Mansfield's style; others will enjoy the sense of control in it.

Repetition is a characteristic of most writers' style. Through the repetition of words from sentence to sentence, sometimes within a single sentence, and by positioning them as she does in her sentences, Mansfield conveys a *tone* and a rhythm of feeling that suggests the sort of person Miss Brill is and how she feels about the experiences she is having. Every aspect of the story is prefigured in not only the elements but also the style of the initial paragraph. Mansfield deliberately repeats not only key words—"sky," "chill," "fur," "little eyes," "little rogue," "sad," "something" —but also, for rhythm, minor words—"from," "when."

When writers *condense* raw material, *concentrate* upon carefully selected elements, and make their style *concise*, they create a *tension* that translates language into physical and psychic events that *happen* to the reader. Mansfield's style, including even her use of commas and dashes, not only conveys information, it affects the reader physically and stimulates psychic responses below the conscious level, so that the style itself is part of what happens to us as we read.

One of the techniques that keeps a reader moving from one sentence to another is *pace*; and even within sentences, the master of style can keep a sense of movement going, thus making style energize action. "But he shook his head, lighted a cigarette, slowly breathed a great deep puff into her face, and, even while she was till talking and laughing, flicked the match away and walked on." To sustain a sense of movement even *within* the style, writers will try, within a single sentence, to cause one thing to *impinge* upon another. Mansfield makes the verbs, "shook," "lighted," "breathed," "talking and laughing," "flicked," and "walked," impinge progressively upon each other; the *syntax* of the sentence (the structuring of phrases), the verbs and the commas themselves, along with what they describe, act upon you, the reader.

But stylistic lapses can impede this sensuous flow of language, as when the author stops to deliver an *abstraction*. There may be times—certainly in "Battle Royal"—when an abstract statement is necessary and "right," partly because Ellison opens with abstractions as a deliberate preparation: "I had some misgivings over the battle royal." But more often abstractions betray somehow, somewhere, a stylistic failure on the part of the writer. Does O'Connor really need to tell us, "He and the grandmother discussed better times"? "Go in fear of abstractions," the imagist poet Ezra Pound said, and he was only saying in different words what Chekhov said about the art of storytelling: the first principle is to *show* not *tell*. O'Connor has already dramatically shown what her line above lamely *tells*.

In the revision stages, a writer may spend hours trying to decide whether to put an adjective before or after a noun; a whole morning putting a comma in, as Joseph Conrad did, or taking it out; finding the perfect word to express something; trying to make a few words say a great deal; trying to cut words so that the remaining words connote or imply more effectively; constructing a phrase: all on the assumption that some readers never tire of prose that is well written.

CONTEXT AND IMPLICATION

Nonfiction writers tell you what they mean, as directly, exactly, and clearly as possible. Fiction writers suggest or *imply* what they mean as they *show* you characters in action. The reader, who is caught up in the showing process, often misses what is implied about character and theme. Frustrated, the reader becomes resentful or even hostile. "Why don't writers just come right out and say what they mean?" (By the way, readers often aren't sure what nonfiction writers mean either.)

Dramatizing or showing offers one kind of experience, and telling offers a very different kind; a poor mixture of the two diminishes the power of both. You read nonfiction because you want *information* or ideas presented, with varying degrees of objectivity. You read fiction to immerse yourself in a subjective experience. Writers want that experience to mean something, but they must imply the meaning somehow to avoid distracting you from the illusion of a lifelike experience. This is a dilemma that the writer solves through the technique of *context* and *implication*. This technique is not difficult to understand, and once you grasp it, most of your problems in reading complex serious fiction dwindle away.

You experience this process every day. Suppose you walk into a campus hangout with a friend and you are sure she sees her roommate in a booth in the back where you usually find the two of them, but your friend quickly slides into a booth up front, out of view of her roommate. The external context is *roommate relations*, the general context is *this situation* today. The implication is obvious: your friend is avoiding her roommate for some reason. What reason? "Is that a new blouse?" you ask. "No, I just borrowed it." The implication, in this context, is that she borrowed it from her roommate without permission and doesn't want her to see her wearing it.

When you become confused, disoriented, or frustrated at any point in reading and studying a story, a look at the contexts should restore clarity. (Except when the writer deliberately wants ambiguity.)

For every story, there are *three kinds of contexts*: *external, general*, and *immediate*. The external context of "Battle Royal" is race relations in the South; the general context is the humiliation of young black men by male white leaders in a small town; the immediate context is the context that exists at any given moment in a story, as in this passage: "I wanted to deliver my speech more than anything else in the world, because I felt that only these men could judge truly my ability, and now this stupid clown was ruining my chances." Suppose you don't quite understand why the narrator is making this statement? If you recall the general context of race relations in the South, the historical framework of it, and the fact that the narrator is looking back after twenty-years, and if you consider the general context of white-black humiliation, and the immediate context—that he is ferociously fighting his own classmate for the amusement of these men—this passage has many ironic implications: the narrator fails to see how profoundly whites have controlled his conception of black-white relations; even after he has seen them drunkenly and licientiously degrade themselves and then maliciously ridicule him and his race, he fails to see that no matter what he does, they will never recognize his worth as an individual. Why doesn't *he* understand, as *you* do? The general context includes a twenty-year distance; the implication is that the narrator, who *now* understands, wants to tell about his behavior at a time when he did *not* understand. He wants you, through the device of context and implication, to see now what he failed to see *then*. To imply is more effective than to *tell*.

Beginning with the first crucial paragraph, writers use words to create a context; the general context evolves and becomes more complex as the reader moves from paragraph to paragraph toward the end. Each literal statement works within the general context, and within the immediate context of each sentence, to enable writers to imply what they cannot or do not want to state explicitly.

Context and implication derive from an author's control of point of view and style. Whatever the point of view, writers rely on contexts to enable them to use implication, and implication enables the reader to participate. Because she uses an omniscient narrator, O'Connor need not rely on context and implication as heavily as Ellison does. On the other hand, Mansfield, who uses the central-intelligence point of view, relies heavily on context and implication. The writer is forced, in the central intelligence mode, to use implication because there are many things she cannot state explicitly, as she could if the point of view were omniscient or first person. Near the end, when the boy asks his girl friend, "Why doesn't she keep her silly old mug at home?" Miss Brill does not at that very moment decide to stay home after this encounter; because Mansfield is confined to Miss Brill's perceptions, she cannot *tell* us. Simultaneously, we experience with Miss Brill her emotion of shock, while catching, in context, the implication of the boy's cruel question: that the consequence of this shock will be that she will never return to the park.

Stories in which everything is clearly, literally shown, or in which writers both show and comment on what they show, are not very interesting. Once you understand how context and implication work, your enjoyment of the story will flow from your awareness of what is implied from paragraph to paragraph. You are involved in the process and involvement increases interest. For analogy, consider the way a joke gets a laugh. If we tell a joke and then *explain* the point, we ruin the effect.

"In the greatest fiction," said Flannery O'Connor, "the writer's moral sense coincides with his dramatic sense." What the writer dramatically shows already embodies the theme or meaning; there is no necessity for adding or tacking on a generalization about that shown experience. Logic, reason, argument are the best means of making a reader *understand* an abstract idea; but the fiction writer wants you to *feel* an idea *as you are having* an emotional, imaginative experience. In the context of a fictional experience, an abstraction or generalization is far less accurate than an implication. The context of the experience evokes the idea.

Context and implication not only generate meaning, they also generate emotion and imagination. The black narrator of "Battle Royal" is speechless with gratitude to the white men who praise and reward him. "A rope of bloody saliva forming a shape like an undiscovered continent drooled upon the leather and I wiped it quickly away." The historical external context of race relations and the general context of white humiliation of blacks in the ballroom enables the reader to grasp, consciously or unconsciously, the implication of the simile "like an undiscovered continent"; as we reluctantly share his emotion of gratitude and pride, we feel our own emotion, remembering the bloody fight, and we feel pathos for all blacks, living and dead, who suffered from the white man's *discovery of the continent* of Africa, and in a kind of flood of intuition, we *imagine* perhaps this young man as a direct descendent, who now tries to "wipe away" this bloody emblem of his people's history and plight.

A paradox of fiction is that emotions (sadness, anger, fear) cannot be communicated to you the reader directly; they can only be implied; in context, implication stimulates the emotion in you. In life, if you tell a friend you are sad, your relationship, with its history, your physical presence, your tone of voice, *may* make him feel that sadness. But if you say nothing about your sadness, if you simply sit for hours staring out a window, sunk in upon yourself, your eyes dull, your voice weak, your friend will empathize far more keenly.

The writer must provide images, rhythm, tone, irony, contrast and other devices to aid you in your response to implications. When Mansfield creates a context by telling you that Miss Brill usually bought a honey-cake at the baker's but that she passes it up today, that is Mansfield's indirect way of conjuring up in you the sadness Miss Brill feels as she passes by the baker's. Your *imagination* is stimulated to see Miss Brill's future life, confined to her cupboard of a room.

In the act of setting up and developing contexts, the writer writes *you* into the process; without your participation, nothing happens. Implications are worthless if the reader fails to respond. When you do respond, you complete the creative process.

AMBIGUITY

Readers sometimes complain of "missing" implications. It may help to note two reasons for this failure to "catch" implications: the reader takes words and sentences too literally and thus fails to respond to a context that the writer has carefully prepared to evoke an implication; or the reader fails to see that the writer has carefully juxtaposed two elements so that they imply a third. Implications arise out of contexts and juxtapositions. If the readers will, then, be aware of the way the writer creates a context or juxtaposes one element to another, they may be more receptive to implications.

The use of implication, and of the other devices discussed in this section, sometimes creates *ambiguity*. It is in the nature of fiction, of language itself, that a passage may convey more than one implication, more than one ironic or symbolic concept.

It may help to note the sources of ambiguity. Readers who are not yet adept at responding to and describing the effects of these literary devices may themselves cause an ambiguity that frustrates their attempt to respond fully to the story. For instance, a reader's inability to understand how point of view works in "Miss Brill" may produce ambiguous responses at various points in the story. Or writers themselves may handle or mishandle the elements of a story in such a way as to produce unintentional ambiguity. Suppose Mansfield had violated the central intelligence point of view by making her own comments on the insensitive lover near the end. The reader, oriented to Miss Brill's perspective would probably regard Mansfield's comments as ambiguous. Both are examples of *negative ambiguity*, making reading unproductively difficult.

But writers may use devices in such a way as to convey several implications or ironies or symbolic elements in a given passage and thus create a controlled, *intentional ambiguity*. For example, Mansfield *intends* the ending of "Miss Brill" to be ambiguous. As in life itself, the emotion or idea conveyed may be one thing or it may be another, or perhaps both simultaneously.

When you encounter ambiguity, try to determine the source: it may be your own inexperience in reading or the writer's lack of skill, or the writer's deliberate intention to pose several possibilities. A fourth source may be your own sensitivity, imagination, or intelligence, which creates an ambiguity that enriches the story.

* * *

Writers use various *technical devices* (symbolism, irony, comparison and contrast, and so on) to create contexts and implications or to stimulate a specific response from the reader. Devices cause the reader to become involved on more than a surface level; involvement makes the reader's responses richer and more complex, and the effects of the story deeper and more lasting. Various devices enhance the effect upon the reader of the elements and techniques discussed in earlier sections. Some of the most important and frequently used of these fictional devices are discussed below.

CONTRAST AND COMPARISON

Contrast and *comparison* are simple devices that enable writers to call your attention to various elements in their stories and enable you to experience them more keenly.

Contrast is a device that helps make us *feel* an experience in fiction. It is to be found in every element of fiction; for instance, conflict sets up a contrast between *protagonist* and *antagonist*.

Contrast helps to set one character off from another by emphasizing what a character is by contrast with what she is not. Irony is one form of contrast. Comparison is a device for emphasizing one thing by showing that it is like another. Metaphor and simile, for example, are forms of comparison.

Contrast lends definition to character. In her superficial preoccupation with manners and morals, the grandmother in "A Good Man is Hard to Find" contrasts with other members of her family and later with the Misfit. There are also points of comparison. Like the grandmother, the Misfit has a highly developed but distorted sense of right and wrong. "Does it seem fair to you, lady, that one is punished a heap and another ain't punished at all?" he asks, right after the mother and the girl are shot.

Sometimes the author moves us from one emotion to a contrasting emotion. The narrator of "Battle Royal" is afraid—and we are afraid for him—as the leaders voice violent opposition to his use of the phrase "social responsibility"; he wants to leave the room, but he also wants to win them over with his speech; he continues, and we feel sorry for him that they ignore him again. "Yet when I finished there was a thunderous applause." They give him an award. "I was so moved I could hardly express my thanks." Fear contrasts with gratitude, but we have our own contrasting emotions in reaction: *anger* that he must fear these men and *sorrow* that the price of gratitude is humiliation.

Sometimes the author's understated or exaggerated style contrasts with what it is describing. In "Battle Royal" the narrator says: "She seemed like a fair bird-girl in veils calling to me from the angry surface of some gray and threatening sea. I was transported." The exaggerated literary style, appropriate to the learned narrator twenty years later as he tells us his story, contrasts with the sordid situation and with the character's lack of capacity *then* for such romantic description.

Ellison compares the humiliaton of the young black fighters; he dramatizes that comparision by juxtaposing the white men's violent handling and chasing of the terrified dancer with the very quick transition into the battle royal; the blacks are already terrified by their exposure to a sexually charged incident involving a white woman with white men watching. (By the way, history has made this comparison between sexual exploitation and racial exploitation even more powerful and meaningful. The story appeared in 1947. The feminist movement has thrown around this passage a context that makes it far more meaningful than Ellison is likely to have imagined.)

The basic strategy that Mansfield employs is counterpoint—a pattern of overt and implied contrasts and comparisons. Miss Brill makes some of those contrasts and comparisons herself, between old and young, male and female, animals and people, closed spaces and open spaces; but the reader sees even more, and the implications are often ironic or symbolic: "The old people sat on the bench still as statues." The reader sees that Miss Brill herself will become like a statue; she is later ignored by the young couple as she ignores this old couple; the statue, in the context of this story, is a symbol of death. Ironically, every time Miss Brill sees a contrast between herself and another person, we see a comparison.

SYMBOLISM

Unless readers are intimately, intricately, and actively in volved in the process of reading, they may not respond to the writer's use of such devices as *symbol, allusion,* or *irony.* These devices provide an added dimension, a necessary complexity to

literary stories. Passive readers who react only to literal statements deny themselves the richer effect and meaning symbolism
and irony provide.

In making use of symbols, literature follows life, which relies, almost every waking moment, upon conscious or unconscious response to signs and symbols. In literature, a symbol is a
word or phrase that has first, a literal meaning. The letters r-o-s-e
signify *rose* and the word signifies a particular flower. But in a
special context, another meaning of *rose* is an *established symbol*
of romantic love. Further, it could also be a symbol of something
else, depending upon how and where it is used in a specific story.

Why use symbols? If you were to ask, why use symbols in
life? the answer would be, because they have become a natural
part of everyday life. Most objects in everyday use are both literal
and symbolic: seven o'clock signifies "get up and go to class";
soap is a symbol of cleanliness; orange juice signifies health; a
coat and tie are symbolic of formality; a key may signify a car
and a car may be a symbol of prestige—or humiliation; skull and
crossbones signify "don't drink this stuff"; green signifies "go" or
symbolizes Spring; road signs signify stop or don't pass; sunshine
is symbolic of cheerfulness, rain of melancholy. On a broader
plane: purple is symbolic of royalty; the cross of Christianity;
the American flag of America; white and black hats, of the good
guys and the bad guys; lilies of death; a star of hope, perhaps
religious hope.

If symbolism is such an everyday thing, why does its use in
literature cause difficulty, obscurity, or ambiguity? One of the
reasons is that most readers approach fiction as they do nonfiction, expecting to be told everything. And they are looking for a
clear story line. They come then to the story in a literal frame of
mind and quite naturally miss symbolic references. Keep in mind
that there are literal commercial stories and symbolic stories, and
that not all serious stories are deliberately symbolic; even so, it
is in the nature of fiction that it is all, to some extent, symbolic,
because symbols are the essence of language. Symbolism is simply one form of literary expression. A symbol helps a writer to

compress many things into one; it adds to the complexity of the work, and complexity is a positive attribute of serious fiction, because it engages all our faculties intensely.

Another source of difficulty for the unwary reader is that writers often use those symbols of everyday life, and those more general established symbols, especially of religion, in special new contexts. They sometimes use them to symbolize an opposite for ironic effect; or they use those familiar symbols in a loose way. The reader becomes confused.

Mansfield makes a simple use of death symbolism in "Miss Brill." The box that contains the fox fur becomes, in context, a symbol, integral to *this* story, of a coffin, and not much more (*how* much more?). It also symbolizes Miss Brill's room, which is like a cupboard, a simile set up in an earlier context through her own perception: "They were odd, silent, nearly all old, and from the way they stared they looked as though they'd just come from dark little rooms or even–even cupboards!"

O'Connor, in "A Good Man Is Hard To Find," reverses established Christian symbols for ironic effect. She creates an ironic context in the first half of the story with the grandmother's hypocritical, self-serving preoccupation with manners and morals; when the Misfit enters, she shifts to religion by ironic contrast: the Misfit is serious about Christianity but in perverse ways. That the ditch is symbolic of the grave is made rather obvious when O'Connor refers to the Misfit's "big black battered hearse-like automobile." Does the Misfit symbolize Death then? "There were three men in it." Why three? Does the Misfit, we may wonder later, symbolize Christ between the two thieves on the cross? Does the ditch then symbolize not just death but Golgotha where Christ was crucified?

In life, symbols are most effective when they clearly stand for something; but in literature, symbols are most effective when they may work in several ways at once. All these meanings can work at once in O'Connor's story without contradicting each other, partly because she uses these symbols ironically. These characters (who use symbols) are confused and perverse, thus the symbols used to represent them are, too. The rescuers do not save, rather they condemn the accident victims. "Christ" brings not life but death—except for the grandmother, who has one brief moment of revelation and grace. For her, the Misfit functions as many things at once: The Devil and Death and Christ and life, her son, herself, her double.

The effect of symbols is usually intellectual, conveying abstract ideas; but sometimes they convey general emotions. Symbols may stimulate not one idea or emotion but two or three or more. So O'Connor creates a special use for several established symbols, all with ironic effects. The plantation is both an established symbol of the Old Antebellum Deep South and all it was and stood for *and* a symbol, integral to *this* story, of superficial, clichéd ideals of a decadent past.

Here are a few suggestions for dealing with symbolism:

1. Try to *avoid* reading everything on a *literal* level. The literal reader suspects that writers don't really use symbols, that teachers read them into the story. If you become aware of the *contexts* and their implications you will be less likely to take everything literally.

2. Try to *avoid hunting* for symbols (symbol mongering) where they do not exist. Here, too, the contexts and their implications will suggest when you are doing that. Symbolism is just another device; not all writers use symbols, although some writers unconsciously include them because, as I have shown, they come naturally in everyday living and in the act of writing.

3. Ask whether a *simile or metaphor* is *only* that and not a symbol. One element that simply parallels another, motifs, for example, are often mistaken for symbols. The writer may have simply emphasized an object in special, nonsymbolic way, by repeating it. Look at the *contexts*.

4. Be careful to read and then *describe the symbol* and its function *accurately*. Some symbols are Freudian, some mythic, some historical, some religious. Don't free associate; symbols are used to achieve precision, even when they are deliberately

ambiguous. On the other hand, try to avoid describing their function too narrowly.

ALLUSION

An allusion is a direct or an indirect reference to something. A writer may allude *to an external context*, as Ellison does when he has the narrator refer to his battle royal opponent as a "stupid clown," a reference to the historical view some whites have that the Negro male is a clown, an entertainer for whites. Was that really Ellison's intention? When the narrator says, near the very end, "That night I dreamed I was at a circus with him [his grandfather] and that he refused to laugh at the clowns no matter what they did," our first assumption is confirmed. We are also aware of other allusions to blacks in the entertainment world, including, of course, boxing, along with the movies ("as a camera sweeps in a reeling scene," in a boxing movie), and, of course, dancing.

The writer may also allude to something *within the story itself*, as Ellison does when he uses the simile "like drunken dancers" to describe the blindfolded fighters; the allusion is to the blond naked woman dancer who precedes the fighters. The purpose of both types of allusions is to lend an added dimension and richer meaning and effect to the story.

Many of the allusions writers employ are *literary*: a reference in one literary work to another literary work. O'Connor alludes to Margaret Mitchell's Civil War novel *Gone With the Wind*. When John Wesley asks his grandmother, "Where's the plantation?" she alludes jokingly to the novel, and probably to the movie as well: "Gone With the Wind.... Ha. Ha." O'Connor alludes to other popular culture media. "She wouldn't stay home to be queen for a day," says June Star, alluding to a popular television program. John Wesley's name is an ironic religious allusion to John Wesley, founder of the Methodist denomination who was saved as a child from a fire and who felt a fire in his heart at his conversion; O'Connor's John Wesley will not be saved from gunfire and he is nowhere near a religious conversion.

Writers may also allude to other art media, other art works. Or they may allude to mythic characters and events. The grandfather's exhortation, "let 'em swaller you till they vomit or bust wide open," in "Battle Royal," *might* be an allusion to Jonah and the Whale. Ellison makes many allusions to the history of black-white relations. "I give up my gun back in the Reconstruction" is a direct allusion to the period following the Civil War. "And yet I am no freak of nature, nor of history" the narrator assures us; in a way, he is, or was, of course; but in a way, he *isn't*, because we are *all* invisible, to ourselves and to each other.

Today, at a time when readers share so small a body of knowledge about history, myth, art, literature, even popular culture, writers use allusion less frequently than did earlier writers. When you encounter a word or phrase that seems ambiguous, that you cannot anchor in the experience you are having as you read, ask yourself whether the writer might be alluding to something; then consider the internal and external context. Almost daily, you have this problem of ambiguous allusion when two friends refer to something they have talked about or experienced without you; you draw on various contexts and sometimes you "figure out" what they mean. You make such allusions yourself; a friend will ask, "What in the world are you alluding to?" You tell her, and she replies, "Okay, I get it now."

IRONY

In the most general sense, *irony* is a recognition of a disparity between what one expects and what actually occurs. The key words in this definition are "recognition" and "one." Who recognizes? Who expects? The person who expects may not be the person who recognizes. "John thinks he's funny, but we all know he's a bore," says Bill. John expects to be taken as funny but it is Bill and "we," not John himself, who recognize that he is not. This example suggests why we enjoy irony: it gives us a delicious sense of power in *knowing*; even if the irony is bitter, knowledge is power; ignorance of the irony, we see, could have made us ridiculous or weak.

In life and in literature, irony helps us see things in one kind of perspective: a detached, critical perspective. An ironic view of life recognizes life's contradictions, incongruities, ambiguities and paradoxes. Mere sarcasm is often mistaken for irony, but it is closer to paradox. "You're very funny," Bill told John, sarcastically. Paradoxically, John may indeed be very funny for reasons not obvious to Bill or his friends; for instance, the *implications* of John's unfunny jokes may be funny.

Students of literature often miss irony because writers use it in ways that are highly complex and unfamiliar. Paradoxically, those same students may respond quite readily to life's ironies and state some of them themselves. "How ironic!" "Ironically . . . " "I don't mean to be ironic . . . " (meaning one does mean to be ironic). In life, when someone says to you, "Don't you see the irony?" you consciously or unconsciously turn to some sort of context for clearer vision. For example, suppose you are shocked to hear Bill say John is not funny, he's a bore; you've always thought John was very funny. But suddenly, you recall the context for John's performances—parties, where he steps up to a large group, launches into one of his routines; you now recall that people usually drift away, leaving you and John together; you realize you like John for reasons other than his humor; painfully, you realize that you often repeat John's jokes or "funny" stories. Finally, you have recognized, in context, the irony of John's conception of himself as funny, and, bitterly, you have the revelation that Bill and others may feel the same way you do. Is that why Bill stated the irony to you alone? On the other hand, some people have a natural temperamental inability to recognize and appreciate irony. Fiction provides *one* means of *acquiring* a taste for irony.

The example given above is somewhat complicated but clear. In fiction, an example *that* clear would be too clear, too obvious. Look, for instance, at this example of irony from "Miss Brill": "No doubt somebody would have noticed if she hadn't been there; she was part of the performance after all." Although the general context so far, and the immediate context, might enable you to sense the irony of Miss Brill's thought (we have reason to doubt whether she would be noticed or that she is part of the performance in any one else's eyes), the force of the irony comes later, when the boy and the girl (cast by Miss Brill as hero and heroine) sit down beside her "where the old couple had been." The cruel way they notice her now ("Ah, be off with you!") dramatically shows that she would not be missed, that she is not part of the drama she herself has conceived. The force of this irony depends upon the reader's having kept in mind, consciously or unconsciously, the earlier sentence that prepares for it. We may call it delayed or retrospective irony. It is a simple irony, but the way Mansfield develops it requires both attention and the enjoyment of relating all parts of the story to each other.

An ironic vision of life characterizes much modern serious fiction. Why? Because so many so-called certainties are daily reversed or at least questioned by new developments in modern life or new ideas. "Crime does not pay" will be taken as an ironic statement, in view of the way our justice system now works, or, ironically, doesn't work. Again, when you feel you may be missing something, and suspect it may be some form of irony, consider the *contexts*. Ask yourself whether one of the devices writers use is being employed to produce the irony: contrast, implication, point of view, style (hyperbole or exaggeration, sarcasm, or understatement), symbolism, allusion.

The use of such devices and of the different types of literary irony produces ambiguity. Sometimes the writer intends ambiguity as a means of exploring possibilities; sometimes the writer unintentionally causes ambiguity; quite often the ambiguity is a result of the reader's lack of understanding of the way irony works in fiction.

Here are five types of ambiguity, with examples from the three stories:

1. *Verbal irony* is saying one thing and meaning another. The writer and the reader share a knowledge of the actual meaning. Sometimes the author's style conveys an ironic attitude or tone that colors the reader's responses. The opening paragraphs of "Battle Royal" clearly set up such an attitude and tone; in this

case, the narrator, as main character, is aware of the irony in his life: "I was looking for myself and asking everyone except myself questions which I, and only I, could answer." The battle royal episode in his young manhood is a prime example of what he means; he was ignorant then of the ironic *implications* of everything he thought, said, and did, ignorant of the almost total *context* of irony in which he lived "during those days." The older self has an ironic perspective as he tells about the younger self. In the context already prepared, "It was a triumph for our whole community" is a prime example of verbal irony; it becomes increasingly ironic as Ellison develops the context. But following that statement, the narrator gives his younger self's perspective, relying on the reader's awareness of the context to produce a flood of ironies by implication.

2. *Dramatic irony* is saying or doing something in ignorance of its opposite meaning. The author shares with the reader a knowledge of the disparity, while the characters may remain ignorant. In context, the grandmother is ignorant of the actual meaning of the phrase she uses, "A good man is hard to find." O'Connor's title would carry the sense the grandmother intends if it did not apply to the ironic fact that *none* of the men in the story are good men. The overwhelming irony of O'Connor's title statement is that good man*kind* is hard to find because of original sin. Ironically, when the grandmother *finds* (and it is her fault they go down this road where they find the Misfit) a man she deceitfully calls "good," he proves to be a very "hard" man. The various ironic implications of the title are *delayed* until O'Connor has developed the various contexts; the final irony is that the Misfit is a good man in his function of forcing the grandmother into a revelation that all men are brothers in sin, and she has a moment of compassion for his spiritual anguish and her own; ironically, this "good" man then shoots her.

The grandmother is ignorant of the reverse application and ironic implication of almost everything she says and does. Bailey, too, fails to recognize the irony of his statement that "This is the one and only time" he will stop for sightseeing. The mother says, "We'll all stay in the car," never realizing that they will never really leave the car except to die. She also says, after the accident, "Maybe a car will come along," and it does, bringing not rescue but death. With *dramatic irony*, there is a contrast between what characters say and how readers apply, at the moment or later, what is said.

3. *Situational irony*, or irony of circumstance, is the presentation of *events* as being the opposite of what one expects or of what ought to be. Ellison's narrator as a young man expected to enlighten the best men of his community; the actual situation is that he is forced to entertain them and that they prove to be the worst of men. He expects to prove to the white leaders with his speech that he is superior to other blacks; the actual situation is that he must prove with his fists that he is not inferior to his classmates. "Perhaps," he thinks in expectation, "I will stand on the rug to deliver my speech." The actual situation is that he must dance on that rug to avoid electrocution as he scrambles for money that turns out to be fake. Ellison ironically juxtaposes the humiliation on the electrified rug to humiliation on the same floor as the young man delivers his speech about humility in the black man's relationship with whites. The reader who fails to keep in mind the fact that the narrator *now*, twenty years later, knows the irony of the ballroom events will be very puzzled by the narrator's attitude and behavior when he was young. "Why doesn't the narrator say how awful this situation is?" Because the situation speaks for itself, and the irony gives bite to what the situation expresses.

GENRE: Types of Fiction

It is important to bear in mind the fact that serious fiction has always been written in the genres described below. But commercial fiction thrives on genre, types of fiction: western, crime, spy, science fiction, fantasy, horror, occult, historical romance, gothic romance, humor, adventure. This interest is reflected in everyday life when you say, "I've got a hard luck story to tell you," or "It's a real success story," or "Here's a funny story," or "This is a really weird story," or "It's a sad story" (Ford Madox Ford's *The Good Soldier* begins: "This is the saddest story I have ever heard"). There is a strong, loyal readership that thrives on each genre of fiction. Why? Those readers enjoy hearing the same story over and over again, delighting in the variations each new example provides. It is a craving that even the most sophisticated readers sometime enjoy satisfying. The reader who prefers commercial fiction seldom ventures into serious fiction, but the reader of serious fiction occasionally ventures into one or two of the genre fictions.

The advantage of genre fiction for the writer and the appeal for the reader is intensity of focus and response. Ease in writing and reading is another appeal. And it is easy to market genre fiction; that ease increases its prevalence. For the devotee of each genre there are no serious limitations, but serious readers find most genre fiction too limited in character development, thematic depth, and artistic range. They want their reading experience to involve them in complex ways; the simplicity of genre fiction can offer only superficial responses for them.

THE TALE

"Tell me a story," is a very early plea in the history of mankind. That plea and the storyteller's compulsion to tell a story produced folk-tales, legends, and myths. In a tale the emphasis is on the story more than on character or meaning, although a moral or message may be tacked on at the end. At the heart of the tale is usually a bizarre incident, either one that *could* happen or one that could not. Homer and other story *writers* set down in writing tales that had been passed on orally from generation to generation. Early writers tried to retain both the substance and techniques of oral storytelling. But telling a tale and writing one, listening to a tale and reading one, are very different kinds of processes and experiences.

Oral storytellers imagine the response of listeners to the simple stories they tell; writers of stories imagine the responses of readers, but their immediate interest is in imagining their character's response to the incidents. In a way the storyteller's listeners become the storywriter's characters. Jane Eyre in Charlotte Bronte's novel says, "the eagerness of a listener quickens the tongue of a narrator"; and to sustain that listener eagerness, the narrator must use various techniques and devices. How does the writer of tales stimulate eagerness in a reader? What is the relationship between the teller and the tale and the teller and the reader? How is the crucial technique of point of view employed in the tale? Consequently, how does the style differ in the tale from the three stories reprinted in this book?

Still another aspect of the tale that may appeal to us is its artistry. Early tales were told, of course, not written, but the storyteller used many techniques that later writers of fiction adapted and employed in more sophisticated, complex ways. You might look then at these tales for simpler uses of the techniques you have been studying so far: point of view, style, symbolism, and so on. Just as the commercial stories offer clear illustrations of basic techniques, these tales offer a slightly different opportunity for comparison, with the focus more intensely on the story. How do the techniques and devices of the tale differ from those of popular and serious stories?

The style is determined by the genre, the tale, the type of tale, the use of fantastic and/or ordinary detail, the intent (to delight, to frighten, to satirize), and the point of view.

In an increasingly complex and frustrating world, a simple story and a clear-cut, predictable plot structure (introduction of the problem, development, climax) satisfy a profound need for simple pleasures. The tale also allows us to keep in touch with the repressed but never vanquished child in us. For some readers of complex modern literature, the very simplicity of the tale makes it inaccessible—our acquired interest in the complex and the profound renders some of us unresponsive to blatant simplicity.

The same writer who wrote one of the greatest modern epics in world fiction, *War and Peace*, also set down many legends because the tale, as a type of story, appealed to him. "A bishop was sailing for Archangel to the Solovetsk Monastery, and on the same vessel were a number of pilgrims on their way to visit the shrines at that place," begins Tolstoy's "The Three Hermits, An Old Legend Current in the Volga District." Most tales begin in that way, or with some variation on a far-away time and place set-up: "Once upon a time in a land far away, three hermits set sail on a pilgrimage."

Our dreams are full of exotic settings, fantastic adventures, strange creatures, wish fulfillments. Mankind has always been fascinated by dream images. Storytellers seemed to combine the bizarre elements of dreams with actual unusual events. Listeners enjoyed the thrill, fear, terror of translating the storyteller's spoken words into images; they also enjoyed the sheer display of imagination in the storyteller. To most people, imagination means the ability to make up what is not real. The storyteller sometimes turned people into animals, animals into people, adapting real events or other wild tales. American frontier storytellers exaggerated bear hunts or barroom brawls in what we call *tall-tales*. Primitive wonder and awe, not just entertainment or instruction, were the feelings listeners of tales experienced. And they enjoyed experiencing the same plot formulas repeatedly. Writers have tried, in literary tales, to retain some of those elements and techniques and reader responses.

HUMOR

There is general agreement that humor is difficult to define, partly because its psychological origins are ill-defined, and partly because there are so many types of humor: gentle humor, satire, farce, slapstick, parody, lampoon, burlesque, etc. Because it is so difficult to write humor of value, it is rare in literary fiction. Humorous fiction, like a joke, relies upon the mechanism of expectation and reversal of expectation, or *surprise*. But there is some serious purpose for humor in a literary short story.

In humor, we simultaneously identify with a character and feel superior; the distance of superiority enables us to laugh at weaknesses in ourselves. *Inferiority* or defeat, is, then, an essential element in humor: contrast between what ought to be and what is expected and what is. There may be a contrast in tone—between the author's deliberately understated style and the importance of the subject matter or between the author's exaggerated style and a trivial subject matter.

One kind of contrast in humor is *irony*. The contrast may be stated or, more often, implied. The author develops a context for implications.

The reader's response may be sympathetic and tolerant laughter or a laughter that criticizes or ridicules, as in *satire*. *Wit* is an intellectual form of humor; our delight may cause us to laugh or to feel a kind of cerebral glow.

SATIRE

One form of humor, satire, provides us with a perspective on faults in attitudes, values, and behavior that we share with all human beings. But satire is a major, distinct and serious literary form of humor in which the author targets specific individuals or type of individuals, or institutions, or governments, or philosophies that need to be reformed. The major weapon of satire is ridicule through something more than mere sarcasm. Our laughter is bitter and scornful, contemptuous, malicious. The author's intent is to provoke us into intolerance of some kind of abuse, so that we will change our attitudes and our actions. The satirist exaggerates to force us to see ills or evils that we try not to see. Satire may be so bitter that laughter is not one of our responses. The goal of good-natured humor is amusement; the goal of satire is reform.

ALLEGORY

In an allegory, persons, places, objects, and actions stand for abstractions—social, religious, political, or philosophical ideas or ideals. The concrete represents the abstract. The setting and time may be actual (historical), fictional (based on reality), or fabulous (purely imagined). Allegory differs from symbolism in that allegory presents very clearly characters and events that represent rather simple abstractions in a simple story. The classic example in fiction is John Bunyan's *Pilgrim's Progress*; in recent years, a fine example is George Orwell's *Animal Farm*, in which the main characters are animals who represent opposing political ideals. Symbolic allegory is one type of allegory; others are parable, fable, beast epic, and satirical.

FANTASY

Allegory always has a strong thematic purpose, but a fantasy may be of two types, *escape* or *serious*. Escape fantasy offers the reader *another* world to be enjoyed purely for its own sake, on its own terms. Serious fantasy offers *another* world as one way of experiencing this world in another dimension and as a way of interpreting it. To be effective, both types must convince the reader that the *other* world is plausible and consistent *on its own terms*. The question is, how thoroughly and how well do its elements obey the other world's own laws? The other world may resemble this one in many ways, but the criteria for judging the author's achievement in creating the fantasy do not come from this world, from our conception of reality. The characters and the events must obey the nature of things as the author has imagined them.

Like allegory, serious fantasy tries to convey a meaning, but the meaning may be as complexly presented as it is in realistic fiction, and all the devices of symbolism and irony, context and implication may be at work in it. The reader's problem is to take these strange creatures and places and events seriously. One kind of fantasy tries to disrupt reality as we know it; the people and places are familiar, but one element of fantasy throws everything into a radically different perspective.

If a writer's purpose is to say something serious about reality why choose to do it in the fantasy genre? One answer is that writers are always trying to imagine ways of giving readers new perspectives on our lives, and fantasy is one of those ways.

HORROR AND OCCULT

The horror or occult tale goes back to man's most primitive stages. A communal fire, the moon overhead, the wind in the trees, the dark, the distant sounds of wild animals, the ghosts of ancestral dead—these were the common and natural, and supernatural, props of the ancient storyteller, whose listeners attributed all kinds of power for good and evil to those very elements. The storyteller's tale, often acted out with song and dance, gave his people a means of confronting fearful forces and defeating them vicariously through the hero or, if the prevailing view of life was more fatalistic, valiantly *failing* to defeat them. Modern humanity is not free of primitive fears; we, too, need to simplify our fears, embody them in a monster, conquer them through a hero, or succumb to them as victims; and when we scream, we laugh to prove we are modern, but we *do* scream, and a scream and a laugh, in this context, are not totally different. The appeal of horror and occult tales is not simply that they satisfy a desire for a cheap thrill; they satisfy something deeper, more complex. But we need the illusion that "it's only a story, or only a movie, it's not real, you know."

HISTORICAL

All readers (and remember, we are a tiny minority of the total adult population) have some sense of history, some desire to know where we, as a people, or mankind, came from, how we got where we are. The commercial historical fiction genre satisfies that need for a broader range of readers more than professional histories do. *Gone With The Wind* is clearly a good example. Readers like to feel that the writer has drawn accurately on the labors of those professionals and they enjoy having the story of the Civil War, for instance, spiced up with imagined characters, a "love interest," and a fast-paced narrative line. This is one of the few popular genres that serious writers have not utilized as often as one might expect, especially when one considers the demonstrated importance of historical cause and effect and the penalty for failing to learn from it.

THE WESTERN

The Western genre has a curious history in prose and in the movies. It began in cheap paperback editions and had wide appeal because it brought back East the news about life in the Great Wild West that few people could visit in person. Stage plays set in the West were popular for the same reason, and more respectable, reaching a different clientele. Its appeals were an exotic place, (the wide open spaces), exotic and new types of heroes (cowboys) and villains (Indians and outlaws) and heroines (the rare Eastern lady among red and white savages), exotic animals, and unusual events. Reading a Western or seeing one on stage, you could venture into a new world. Gradually, hardcover novels by good or competent writers—Bret Harte, Owen Wister—appeared.

Then it seemed that the Wild West was vanishing; the Indians had been subjugated and confined to reservations, the buffalo was almost obsolete, and the railroad and farmers were bringing stability and law and order. Now Westerns offered stories about a fabled American past when the last free individuals roamed the West. And a new medium rescued the genre: the movies, with actors and the heroes they played seeming to be one and the same in this awesome convincing, life-like medium. A small but loyal readership of men kept the genre alive in cheap paper and hardcover formats, but for decades the general public was primarily drawn to the western in the film medium. Violent resolutions of clear-cut moral issues—a man, a gun, a horse—were very appealing. Today, the western in both media is almost extinct, kept alive by a few good writers like Louis L'Amour. Only a few literary writers, for instance, Walter Van Tilburg Clark (*The Ox-Bow Incident*) or Larry McMurty (*Lonesome Dove*), have written westerns.

CRIME

The crime genre offers two general types: the *detection* story, made popular by Edgar Allen Poe, in which the emphasis was on intellect; out of that type, at a time when the English genteel story of crime detection ("The Butler did it") dominated the scene there emerged the distinctively American type, the hard-boiled private detective type of crime story. The hard-boiled type was hammered out at one cent a word for the pulp magazine *Black Mask* by Dashiell Hammett. The emphasis here is not on intellect but on violence, the setting not the English country manor house but the mean streets of San Francisco and New York.

Crime fiction's appeal is much like that of the Western: the solitary hero (adrift in the concrete jungle of the big cities instead of the wide open spaces), armed with only his gun, behind the wheel of his battered car (instead of astride his faithful horse). He is a kind of knight, but unlike the Western hero, he sometimes does not treat women gently, even though he, too, may rescue them.

Readers liked seeing the realities of everyday life dealt with in an ideal way, by a hero who could act decisively, outside the law, as the Western hero often did. But the detective hero was closer to readers than the Westerner was. And he spoke their language. In fact, a distinctive feature of the hardboiled private eye story was that it was usually told in the first person by the private eye, using the slang of the street. Both heroes are men of few words, but the private eye gives a kind of concise report on his cases. Most Western writers choose the omniscient point of view as if they had created this strange world out West themselves and needed the fullest kind of style, an elevated style to match the grandeur. In the crime story, the pace, like the hero's mode of transportation, is much faster than in the Western.

SCIENCE FICTION

Science fiction is to be distinguished from pure fantasy in that it utilizes present scientific achievements as a basis for imagining scientific discoveries in the future, usually enabling man to explore, colonize, settle, and govern other worlds in space. The outer spaces of science fiction remind one of the wide open spaces of the old West, but the two types seem to appeal to very different, though basically romantic, temperaments. Science fiction is to the Atomic Age what the Western was to the late Industrial Revolution at the turn of the century. With their indulgence in the imagination as it takes flight into the historical past or the prophetic future from a basis in fact, both types are essentially romantic.

Psychological analysis and supernatural speculation characterize some of these novels. As the projections of early science fiction novelists become everyday realities and as novelists working in this type today use visions of the future to make serious comments on social and political problems of the present, this major popular type is being read more seriously.

The range of this type is quite broad. Mary Shelley's *Frankenstein* (1816) is a Gothic variant that anticipates science fiction. Some of the early classics extrapolate as logically and, as it has turned out, as prophetically as possible from actual scientific knowledge to probable future developments—for example, Jules Verne, *From the Earth to the Moon* (1865) and H.G. Wells, *The War of the World* (1898). Some writers combine conventional elements of fantasy and romance and depict the nearly impossible; some writers use science fiction as a basis for psychological studies or excursions into the supernatural.

Regarded until recently as a subliterary genre, often lurid and overly spectacular, full of clichés in style, stereotyped characters, and stock situations, the science fiction novel has, along with the occult, recently achieved a kind of respectability, even in universities. The various types of science fiction can be used as bases for serious comment on the actual world. Social and political problems are implicit in science fiction. George Orwell's *1984* (1949) combines elements of proletarian fiction with anti-Utopian futurism; it may be termed more a prophetic than a science fiction novel of the usual sort. Aldous Huxley's *Brave New World* (1932) is a somber satire of utopias; Anthony Burgess's *A Clockwork Orange* (1962) and Kurt Vonnegut's *Slaughterhouse Five* (1970) and *Cat's Cradle* (1963) are black humor satires.

A NOTE ON NONCONVENTIONAL FICTION

You have now learned a number of techniques for analyzing and interpreting some of the ways fiction works. But you have also learned that to some degree every story, even the simplest, defies definite interpretation, and that is especially true of *avant-garde*—nonconventional—stories; they seem immune to literary analysis. They are so far outside recognizable contexts that perhaps they cannot be judged good or poor—they simply are. There is an inherent contradiction in trying to explain a story that was originally conceived to defy analysis. All we can expect to do here, then, is suggest a few ways of approaching stories (or "fictions") by avant-garde, experimental, or innovative writers ("fictionists" is the name many prefer).

The stock elements and devices of commercial stories and the genres and techniques of conventional serious fiction are employed in different contexts in *experimental* works.

All art is in a primary sense about itself; every story is about the process of storytelling, about the relationship between the writer and the reader. That is more obvious in experimental than in traditional fiction. Every story offers the reader hints about ways it should be read. One way, then, to gather clues to understanding the work of innovators is to look closely at passages from the fictions themselves.

Experimental writing may prove less incomprehensible if you keep the following pro and con observations in mind. (Not all are true of each work):

PRO
Nonconventional writers:

reject traditional techniques because those techniques fail to depict facets of our contemporary experience;

strive to destroy all art forms and show through their own methods the madness of all human existence: racial, social, and economic inequality, the threat of the bomb, insane wars, and political treachery;

are not afraid to take calculated risks;

strive to be vital, exuberant, and audacious;

attempt to experience phenomena purely, innocently;

break up the surface appearances of everyday life;

explode the barriers between the conscious life and the unconscious life;

have an air of being under the influence of mysterious, mythic forces;

violate preconceptions and expectations about life and art;

are against imitating life—against realism;

aim for a work that does not reflect the real world, but a world of its own, an alternative world;

claim each work is a new thing, a new event, not a report on already finished things and events;

claim that each work is atypical, idiosyncratic, an act of pure creation;

create worlds that exist nowhere beyond the page;

write works that are about the process of their own creation;

write fiction about fiction;

reach for a unique style, using techniques that "shatter syntax";

are against chronological structure and plot, against the elements of conflict, exposition, complication, revelation, resolution;

write fiction that remains unresolved in levels of character, action, and theme;

use popular fiction elements as their material and distort them to outrage the middle class who prefer them;

explore the use of fantasy;

do violence to readers—startle, provoke, disorient, disturb, frighten, alienate them;

force readers to experience relativity in all things;

reach for new forms of extremity;

refuse to impose order upon disorder, force readers to ride the wild horses of chaos;

are against intellectual analysis;

invite readers' free, subjective responses;

claim that willful obscurity may enable the imagination to explore possibilities and push into far-out realms where transformations may occur;

claim that each fiction may extend the possibilities of art and life;

inspire readers' own experimentation in perception and behavior that may change their lives.

CON
Critics of innovative writing declare:

that few of its techniques are really shocking;

that innovative writers are arrogantly subjective, willfully per- verse, self-indulgent, self-conscious, self-righteous;

that they produce claustrophobic, irrational, deranged, and para- noid fictions that reek of futility;

that they write out of destructive, antisocial impulses;

that their dark decadent, amoral, subversive, anarchistic, offen- sively violent, often pornographic, and blasphemous works are abstract, abstruse, arbitrary, ambiguous, bizarre, ob- scure, and lack form, unity, coherence, and control;

that choosing only to be free, their freedom is a self-contradiction; the eclectic writer is much freer to choose, for he or she can skillfully use both conventional and innovative techniques;

that they make pretentious, sometimes hysterical claims of orig- inality in vision and techniques, as if ignorant of the fact that innovation was a feature of fiction for the start.

These stories will seem much less difficult to you on second or third reading. To respond most fully, even readers who crave innovative writing must reread a fiction several times. Just let each fiction happen to you tthe first time you read it. The best way to get into innovative fiction's sometimes murky waters, then, is to plunge from the highest diving board.

CONSIDERATIONS AS YOU READ

The purpose of the *study* of fiction is to develop an ability to respond as fully as possible to every aspect of a story. Re- member, the writer himself had to struggle through the revision process to create the story you are reading. The act of reading that story is also a part of the creative process.

If you become confused, mystified, or disoriented at any point in reading (or, more usefully, *re*-reading) a story, review the following list of considerations. These considerations suggest what you might mark in your text for later discussion and writing review.

1. Every element in a story—character, conflict, plot, theme—is controlled by the way writers handle the *point of view* they have chosen (first person, third person-central intelligence, omniscient).
2. The writer's *style*—the conscious choice of words, the phrasing—is determined by the point of view he or she employs.
3. Beginning with the first crucial paragraph, the writer uses words to create a *context*, which evolves from paragraph to paragraph to the crucial final paragraph.
4. The literal statements work within the overall context, and within the immediate context of any given paragraph, to enable the writer to *imply* what is not explicitly stated.
5. What is implied (or evoked or conveyed indirectly) in a story usually has a more powerful effect than what is obviously stated because *implication* stimulates the reader's own emotions, imagination, and intellect.
6. The reason why writers use various *technical devices* is to create contexts and implications or to stimulate some specific response from the reader; as the reader becomes involved, the reader's experiences become richer and more complex, and the effects are deeper and more lasting.
7. *Contrast* and *comparison* are simple devices that enable the writer to call your attention to his use of symbols and irony, among other things.
8. To respond to the writer's use of a *symbol*, an *allusion*, or to *irony*, a reader must be intimately, intricately, and actively involved in the process of reading and responding; the result is a much richer experience than if the reader where only passively reacting to literal statements.
9. With considerations 1 through 8 in mind, a person who is studying the nature and effect of fiction, as opposed simply to reading it as one usually does, may more fully respond to all the experiences the writer has imagined for the reader.

10. Is the story written in a specific genre? If so, does it depart from the limited elements of that genre? Or does the story draw on aspects of several genres?

CONSIDERATIONS AS YOU DISCUSS

The *purpose of class discussion* is to enable you to evaluate your own emotional, imaginative, and intellectual responses by comparing them with those of your instructor and your classmates. Remember, writers, in writing and rewriting, put themselves through a similar process of exploratory questioning, in the course of which their emotions, imaginations, and intellects discover new possibilities.

The *objective of class discussion* is not to arrive at definite answers—there are few such answers in any discussion of the effect of a work of fiction—but to help make more facets of a story accessible to your responses.

The following list of considerations may help you in class discussion:

1. Think of all comments as relevant, directly or indirectly.
2. Don't assume your responses are less sensitive or informed than your classmates'; most are probably assuming the same about theirs.
3. Try to avoid purely personal responses unless they illustrate considerations that are likely to apply to other readers as well. (As you read, personal responses are, of course, the essence of your experience.)
4. In the course of discussion, if anything about the story or the discussion of it is unclear, ask questions for clarification; others will benefit as well.
5. Try to follow up your statements or questions with further statements and questions, developing, if possible, a sequence that moves from the beginning to the end of the story. Try not to make an assertion or ask a question and then withdraw; pursue a line of inquiry.
6. Stick to the point; don't go off on tangents. When one point is exhausted, move on to another.

7. Be curious and attentive to what's being said. Listen, think about what others are saying. Be a good listener, so you can be a more effective talker.
8. Opinions may or may not be, in themselves, interesting or persuasive, but they are more forceful if they are enhanced by your reference to specifics in the text or by your tracing a pattern of illustrations through the text. (Your annotations of the text will help you here.)
9. Put forth your own ideas, but be flexible, allow yourself to be influenced by what others are saying.
10. Talk concretely, not too abstractly.
11. Build your own thoughts and impressions with the help of others.
12. Try to bring others into the discussion. Ask others what they think about the points you raise.
13. Even when you only ask a question, direct the instructor and students as often as possible to specific pages and passages in the text to make your question clear.
14. Initiate, stimulate, direct, and respond to discussion. Each member of a class is simultaneously a student and a teacher.

MASTER REVIEW QUESTIONS THAT APPLY TO MOST FICTION

Each question one may ask about each story read in introductory courses may be restated in general terms and applied to most (but not all) stories. The questions below mirror the order in which their key topics are discussed in the text. They provide a review of some of the major points for reading, discussion, and writing. I will draw on Flannery O'Connor's "A Good Man Is Hard to Find" to illustrate.

1. Who is the *protagonist*? (The grandmother.)
2. When and where is the *setting*? (Time: the early 1950's. Place: urban and rural Georgia, the Deep South.)
3. What is the *story or plot*? (Story: An average family sets out in a car for a vacation in Florida; when their car wrecks, the Misfit and two other escaped convicts execute the family. Plot: An average family, representing three generations,

deceive, con, and verbally abuse each other as they travel in a car toward Florida; as three escaped convicts politely execute members of the family, the grandmother achieves a moment of grace in her encounter with the Misfit.

4. What is the *conflict*? (The grandmother's superficial manners and ethics conflict with the deep spiritual torment of the Misfit.)

5. What is the *point of view*? (Omniscient, but with a strong focus on the grandmother.)

6. What are the characteristics of the style that derive from the *point of view*? (As omniscient narrator, O'Connor mixes her own complex style with the tone, rhythm, and vocabulary of her characters. Her images are clear, harsh, and comic: "His jaw was as rigid as a horse shoe.")

7. What is the *external context*? (The Deep South and the Christian religion.)
What is the *general context*? (Changing manners and ethics in the urban Deep South; the violent testing of religious values.)
What are some of the most significant *immediate contexts*? (The self-righteous grandmother deceives her family to get her way—to go in search of a plantation. The grandmother tries to con the Misfit out of shooting her, "a lady.")

8. What *other techniques or devices* does the author use?
Comparison and Contrast: (The grandmother and the Misfit, regarding religion.)
Symbolism: (The ditch is a symbol, like a grave, of death; also like Golgotha, a symbol of Christ's crucifixion.)
Allusion: ("Gone With the Wind" is a direct allusion to the Civil War novel and movie.)
Irony: (The children's mother says, "Maybe a car will come along." One does, with an opposite result from what she imagined.)

9. To what *genre* does the story belong (if relevant)? (Southern gothic or grotesque humor or religious allegory.)

10. How do the preceding considerations suggest *theme* or *meaning*? (Each consideration contributes to some facet of the

story's complex, rather ambiguous meaning. *One* way of stating it is: many "good" people play superficial games to avoid experiencing the agony of true religious conversion; some "bad" people react violently to the most profound religious questions. When these two extreme types violently clash, one or both *may*, at the last moment, achieve grace.)

THREE
THE ART OF WRITING
ABOUT FICTION

The elements in this section are based to some extent upon the freshman English course you took not so long ago, adapted to the specific kind of writing done in literature courses.

I have cited "A Good Man Is Hard To Find" often as an example because it illustrates most of the elements and techniques discussed in preceding chapters. I will use it to illustrate the process of writing a paper about fiction.

I offer the author's own interpretation, speaking to her college student readers. I also offer the interpretative comments of another Southern writer who is also a critic, Caroline Gordon. Then I give an example of a student's approach to some of the same elements O'Connor and Gordon discuss: suspense, point of view, and theme.

1
KINDS OF ESSAYS

Knowing that writing an essay is one way to help you shape and focus the ideas you derive from reading, making notations, considering the questions included in text–anthologies, and class discussion, your instructor will assign one or more papers, perhaps choosing from five general kinds of literary essays:

Description
Analysis
Comparison and Contrast
Interpretation
Personal Evaluation or Appreciation

Description

The purpose of a description essay is to show the reader *what* the story is. A description essay does not provide a mere plot summary. For instance, a general objective description of O'Connor's "A Good Man Is Hard To Find" should explain in detail the characters and their relationships, the conflict, the setting, the plot, the meaning.

Analysis

The analysis essay focuses on one aspect of the story, a character, the setting, the theme, the conflict or the use of a major technique or device, such as symbolism or irony.

Comparison and Contrast

For instance, how does one character compare or contrast with another? The home and restaurant and car settings with the ditch? The inner conflict with the external conflict? You might be asked to compare the grandmother with a character in another story, such as the elderly lady in "Miss Brill," or the anonymous narrator in "Battle Royal."

Interpretation

Interpretation of the overall meaning of the story: the emphasis is on theme, with a focus on one element—character, or a technique, point of view, or a device, irony—or one aspect of the over-all meaning, such as hypocrisy or self-delusion.

Personal Evaluation or Appreciation

The personal evalutaion essay is a subjective description of your personal responses to your choice of elements in the story: how did the story affect you? how does it relate to your own life? why did you like or dislike it? what insights into life or literature did it offer you?

These types of writing apply as well to other fields; you probably studied and practiced them in freshman English; your instructor may, therefore, simply give you a choice. The process described below applies as well to one kind of essay as to another.

2
STAGES OF WRITING

Prewriting Activities

Before you begin to write, it is best to take advantage of some prewriting activities out of which your essay may evolve in stages. The assumption here is that you have not let the paper go until the night before class or the hour between calculus and English. Nor, unless permitted to do so, have you consulted published sources.

A. Review Your Resources

If you have practiced some disciplined foresight, you will have already gotten started on your paper (and even later papers) by reading each story three times, marking passages, making *marginal annotations* as you read and during class discussion. Let's suppose you have been assigned or you have chosen to write an *analysis* essay on "A Good Man Is Hard To Find." You turn to it as one steps up to an abyss, to find the story totally unannotated. You read it, but remember little or nothing. You listened to class discussion (or were absent that day) but what was said? But let's suppose you find it heavily annotated. For instance, beside the line "Bailey was the son she lived with, her only son," you may have noted: "the point of view is probably omniscient." Beside "whose face was as broad and innocent as a cabbage," you may have noted: "*tone* seems comic."

Look now at the *questions at the end of the story.* They provide a kind of review of major considerations. For instance, one question might be, "How does the grandmother relate to the family and to other people?" You may have answered this question with a few phrases; this one: "Manipulates them with superficial manners and ethics and with deceit." (If you make direct use of a question in the text, cite it in your paper.)

By this time, you should feel fairly good about the prospect before you. And when you identify notes made on class discussion (perhaps in a different color of ink, so that your own comments make a dialogue with class comments), you might feel rather confident, musing, for instance, over this notation of a question raised by the instructor: "At which points in the story does O'Connor foreshadow the encounter of the family with the Misfit?" This question may have been raised by a classmate; "Does the ditch symbolize anything?" Perhaps your note was: "Ditch symbolizes a grave."

You may see at this point that you are really further along than you perhaps thought. You have something to go on. And suppose the instructor assigned outside reading for added stimulus; you may or may not make use of the essays. (Usually, outside reading is not assigned; many instructors do not want you to consult published material without permission.) You have marked passages with a highliter and made notes in the margin, perhaps as shown below.

Flannery O'Connor on "A Good Man is Hard to Find"

A story really isn't any good unless it successfully resists paraphrase, unless it hangs on and expands in the mind. Properly you analyze to enjoy but it's equally true that to analyze with any discrimination, you have to have enjoyed already, and I think that the best reason to hear a story read is that it should stimulate that primary enjoyment.

I don't have any pretensions to being an Aeschylus or Sophocles and providing you in this story with a cathartic experience out of your mythic background, though this story I'm going to read certainly calls up a good deal of the South's mythic background, and it should elicit from you a degree of pity and terror, even though its way of being serious is a comic one. I do think, though, that like the Greeks you should know what is going to happen in this story so that any element of suspense in it will be transferred from its surface to its interior.

I would be most happy if you had already read it, happier still if you knew it well, but since experience has taught me to keep my expectations along these lines modest, I'll tell you that this is the story of a family of six which, on its way driving to Florida, gets wiped out by an escaped convict who calls himself the Misfit. The family is made up of the Grandmother and her son, Bailey, and his children, John Wesley and June Star and the baby, and there is also the cat and the children's mother. The cat is named Pitty Sing, and the Grandmother is taking him with them, hidden in a basket.

Now, I think it behooves me to try to establish with you the basis on which reason operates in this story. Much of my fiction takes its character from a reasonable use of the unreasonable, though the reasonableness of my use of it may not always be apparent. The assumptions that underlie this use of it, however, are those of the central Christian mysteries. These are assumptions to which a large part of the modern audience takes exception. About this I can only say that there are perhaps other ways than my own in which this story could be read, but none other by which it could have been written. Belief, in my own case anyway, is the engine that makes perception operate.

The heroine of this story, the Grandmother, is in the most significant position life offers the Christian. She is facing death. And to all appearances she, like the rest of us, is not too well prepared for it. She would like to see the event postponed. Indefinitely.

I've talked to a number of teachers who use this story in class and who tell their students that the Grandmother is evil, that in fact, she's a witch, even down to the cat. One of these teachers told me that his students, and particularly his southern students, resisted this interpretation with a certain bemused vigor, and he didn't understand why. I had to tell him that they resisted it because they all had grandmothers or great-aunts just like her at home, and they knew, from personal experience, that the old lady lacked comprehension, but that she had a good heart. The southerner is usually tolerant of those weaknesses that proceed from innocence, and he knows that a taste for self-preservation can be readily combined with the missionary spirit.

This same teacher was telling his students that morally the Misfit was several cuts above the Grandmother. He had a really sentimental attachment to the Misfit. But then a prophet gone wrong is almost always more interesting than your grandmother, and you have to let people take their pleasures where they find them.

It is true that the old lady is a hypocritical old soul; her wits are no match for the Misfit's, nor is her capacity for grace equal to his; yet I think the unprejudiced reader will feel that the Grandmother has a special kind of triumph in this story which instinctively we do not allow to someone altogether bad.

I often ask myself what makes a story work, and what makes it hold up as a story, and I have decided that it is probably some action, some gesture of a character that is unlike any other in the story, one which indicates where the real heart of the story lies. This would have to be an action or a gesture which was both totally right and totally unexpected; it would have to be one that was both in character and beyond character; it would have to suggest both the world and eternity. The action or gesture I'm talking about would have to be on the analogical level, that is, the level which has to do with the Divine life and our participation in it. It would be a gesture that transcended any neat allegory that might have been intended or any pat moral categories a reader could make. It would be a gesture which somehow, made contact with mystery.

There is a point in this story where such a gesture occurs. The Grandmother is at last alone, facing the Misfit. Her head clears for an instant and she realizes, even in her limited way, that she is responsible for the man before her and joined to him by ties of kinship which have their roots deep in the mystery she has been merely prattling about so far. And at this point, she does the right thing, she makes the right gesture.

I find that students are often puzzled by what she says and does here, but I think myself that if I took out this gesture and what she says with it, I would have no story. What was left would not be worth your attention. Our age not only does not have a very sharp eye for the almost imperceptible intrusions of grace, it no longer has much feeling for the nature of the violences which precede and follow them. The devil's greatest wile, Baudelaire has said, is to convince us that he does not exist.

I suppose the reasons for the use of so much violence in modern fiction will differ with each writer who uses it, but in my own stories I have found that violence is strangely capable of returning my characters to reality and preparing them to accept their moment of grace. Their heads are so hard that almost nothing else will do the work. This idea, that reality is something to which we must be returned at considerable cost, is one which is seldom understood by the casual reader, but it is one which is implicit in the Christian view of the world.

I don't want to equate the Misfit with the devil. I prefer to think that, however unlikely this may seem, the old lady's gesture, like the mustard-seed, will grow to be a great crow-filled tree in the Misfit's heart, and will be enough of a pain to him there to turn him into the prophet he was meant to become. But that's another story.

This story has been called grotesque, but I prefer to call it literal. A good story is literal in the same sense that a child's drawing is literal. When a child draws, be doesn't intend to distort but to set down exactly what he sees, and as his gaze is direct, he sees the lines that create motion. Now the lines of motion that interest the writer are usually invisible. They are lines of spiritual motion. And in this story you should be on the lookout for such things as the action of grace in the Grandmother's soul, and not for the dead bodies.

We hear many complaints about the prevalence of violence in modern fiction, and it is always assumed that this violence is a bad thing and meant to be an end in itself. With the serious writer, violence is never an end in itself. It is the extreme situation that best reveals what we are essentially, and I believe these are times when writers are more interested in what we are essentially than in the tenor of our daily lives. Violence is a force which can be used for good or evil, and among other things taken by it is the kingdom of heaven. But regardless of what can be taken by it, the man in the violent situation reveals those qualities least dispensable in his personality, those qualities which are all he will have to take into eternity with him; and since the characters in this story are all on the verge of eternity, it is appropriate to think of what they take with them. In any case, I hope that if you consider these points in connection with the story, you will come to see it as something more than an account of a family murdered on the way to Florida. [1969]

Caroline Gordon and Allen Tate: Comment on O'Connor's "A Good Man Is Hard To Find"

Flannery O'Connor has [an] exquisite ear for the cadences of common every-day speech . . . , but her characters seem to move in the fierce glare of a noon-day sun and her style is . . . lean and hard

Excerpt from *The House of Fiction*, by Caroline Gordon and Allen Tate. Copyright © 1950, 1960 by Charles Scribner's Sons. Reprinted by permission of Farrar, Straus and Giroux, Inc.

like Swift's—if not as distinguished. Her lapses result, seemingly, from her reluctance, or it may be inability, to solve the first problem which confronts any writer of fiction: on whose authority is this story told? Miss O'Connor, as it were, backs off, takes a running jump and lands in the middle of her usually troubled waters. The lay reader is fascinated from start to finish and only an occasional purist will be distressed when he realizes that she is playing fast and loose with an age-old convention; in her stories the Omniscient Narrator, one who, seeing all and knowing all, has immemorially been presumed to be elevated considerably above the conflict, often speaks like a Georgia "cracker."

But it is perhaps captious to apply such a standard to O'Connor's prose, which is, in her hands, a subtle and powerful instrument with which she has achieved effects produced by no other writer of her generation.

In "A Good Man Is Hard to Find," the members of a Southern family are setting out on a vacation trip. The father of the family, Bailey, does not have a "naturally sunny dispositon . . . and trips made him nervous." Bailey seems to be laconic by nature, or it may be that silence is the weapon he uses against his mother's wiles. At any rate, he speaks seldom and then usually in negation of something somebody else has said. The little boy, John Wesley–so many of O'Connor's characters take their names from the Great Revivalist!–seems to have inherited his father's negative attitude towards life and says, "Let's go through Georgia fast so we won't have to look at it much." The mother, whose face is "as broad and innocent as a cabbage," is even more negative in her attitude towards life than her husband and son; she speaks seldom during the story and says, "Yes, thank you" as she is led off to death with her baby on her arm.

The grandmother is the only one who enjoys the trip. The children's mother is wearing slacks and still has her head tied up in a green kerchief but the grandmother has made a careful toilet; "in case of accident any one seeing her dead on the highway would know that she is a lady."

Flannery O'Connor's prose has no "poetic" passages. Indeed, one can say of her style that in general it lacks elevation–the kind of elevation which Logan Pearsall Smith in an illuminative metaphor has characterized as "the far, blue peaks of Helicon" which, he maintains, are always visible on "the horizon" of a great prose writer. Neverthehess, O'Connor's conceptions are poetic in the deepest sense. The grandmother *is* a lady, of high—and as this country goes—incient degree. She represents the Old South.

The Misfit feels the impact of the grandmother's character and personality. The terrible dialogue seems to go on for a long time. But the bond between them snaps–suddenly and dreadfully–when the grandmother recognizes the escaped convict is "one of my babies, one of my own children" and reaches out and touches him on the shoulder. He cannot bear the con-frontation and shoots her through the chest three times.

As for The Misfit, we have met him before, too, in O'Connor's stories. He is of the same breed as Haze Motes, of *Wise Blood*, who preaches the Church of Christ without Christ or as the Bible salesman who uses a different name at every house he calls at and his been "believing in nothing ever since he was born." But whether he is stealing a girl's artificial leg as a souvenir of an attempted seduction or massacring the members of a family on a country road, he has only one preoccupation: theology. Indeed, this modern hero—or villain—concerns himself with only one dogma: the union of the human and divine which theologians call the hypostatic union. The grandmother would have lived longer if she had not uttered the name of Jesus:

> Finally she found herself saying' "Jesus. Jesus," meaning Jesus will help you, but the way she was saying it, it sounded as if she might be cursing.

The Misfit responds promptly:

> Yes'm . . . . Jesus thown everything off balance. If He did what He said, then it's nothing for you to do but thow everything away and follow Him, and if He didn't, then it's nothing for you to do but enjoy the few minutes you got left the best way you can–by killing somebody or burning down his house or doing some other meanness to him. No pleasure but meanness . . . .

The Misfit, like Haze Motes and the Bible saleman, is illiterate, but he is spiritually kin to more highly paced Americans. He denies the existence of Christ but his whole life is given over to speculation on the nature of Christ. The philospher and amateur theologian, the elder Henry James, whom Austin Warren numbers among his "New England Saints," spent his life in a similar preoccupation. The Misfit states his disbelief in words of one syllable: "Jesus was the only One that ever rasied the dead. He shouldn't have done it. He thrown everything off balance." The elder James also rejects the doctrine of the hypostatic union when he speaks of "the venomous tradition of a disproportion between Man and his Maker"; he seems to feel that when God became Man he should not have remained God.

In Flannery O'Connor's vision of modern man—a vision not limited to Southern rural humanity—all her characters are "displaced persons," not merely the people in the story of that name. They are "off center," out of place, because they are victims of a rejection of the Scheme of Redemption. They are lost in that abyss which opens up for man when he sets up as God. This *theological framework* is never explicit in O'Connor's fiction. It is so much a part of her direct gaze at human conduct that she seems herself to be scarely aware of it. This accounts to a great extent for her power. It is a Blakean vision, not through symbol as such but through the actuality of human behavior; and it has Blake's explosive honesty, such as we find in

But most through midnight streets I hear
How the youthful harlot's curse
Blasts the newborn infant's ear
And blights with plague the marriage hearse.

But though the theological framework of Miss O'Connor's stories is never explicit, it is, at the same time, never absent, which would seem to constitute the chief difference between her work and Truman Capote's. His characters move through the same mists of despair and doom but we are not given to understand why they are so fated. There is in his stories no one like "The Misfit," with his crisp, dogmatic explanation of why he is impelled to commit murder: "Jesus thrown everything off balance." [1960]

* * *

You now have O'Connor's own comments on key elements in her story in a situation where she was talking with students who have studied the story and is about to read it to them. Keep in mind that the story itself is the primary authority; the author's comments are authoritative but not definitive, nor necessarily reliable in all respects; Caroline Gordon's comments, those of other critics, your instructor's, and your own have differing kinds of authority. Gordon, keep in mind, is commenting not only as a critic and teacher (her comments are found in one of the best textbooks on fiction, *The House of Fiction,* edited with her poet-critic husband Allen Tate in 1950, second edition in 1960) but as a writer of fiction herself. These essays may provide you with somewhat different perspectives.

B. Make a List of Elements and Ideas

Scanning your various notes, and supplementing with ideas that come to mind under that stimulus, make an unnumbered list of those ideas that appeal to you and that seem to group together. For example:

negative attitudes toward each other—the family members

foreshadowing: Misfit news story

point of view—Omniscient

COMIC TONE—rattled newspaper at Bailey's bald head

Focus on GRANDMOTHER—superficial manners, etc. Hypocrite

Cafe scene—Red Sammy & Wife, negative relationship also

Use of animals—cat and monkey. Cat & Grandmother, Cat & Misfit at end

Grandmother manipulates everybody—used manners and ethic to control people

Misfit again—in cafe—foreshadows

Title–reference in Cafe—"good man" (later with Misfit)

Grandmother *lies* about secret panel

Bad consequences of Grandmother's manipulation—Accident, waves to Misfit, blurts out she recognizes him

SYMBOL = ditch=grave, car=hearse

Irony—killer polite, like grandmother

Grandmother tries to con killer—he speaks truth

Irony—rescuers turn out to be killers

Irony–"pray"—the pistol shot. Prayer not an easy solution

Religious discussion—Christ (see Gordon essay)

Irony—grandmother touches killer out of compassion, he shoots her. *Why?*

Killers say no pleasure but meanness, kills lady who shows compassion, then says, "It's no real pleasure in life." *Why?* Irony.

C. Identify Your Subject

By now, you should be fortified with materials for an analysis essay. But an analysis of what? What is your *subject* to be? If you scan your list, you may identify your subject. For instance, here are some possibilities derived from the list above:

The grandmother and the Misfit
Irony
Symbolism
Religion

Suppose you decide on irony.

D. Narrow your Subject

This step may prove to be difficult. Make another list of narrower approaches:

bitter ironies
point of view and irony
irony and character
irony and violence
irony and religion

Suppose you decide on irony and character.

E. Derive an Outline from Your List of Ideas

Few people really enjoy doing outlines, because now you must organize your thoughts about the subject you have now narrowed, and that is seldom easy. Number in order those ideas on your list that you intend to use in the outline. Clarify and organize your ideas in your mind first, then you might try "mind mapping" those ideas, as shown in the figure on page 136.

Mind Map Outline: "Ironic Characters"

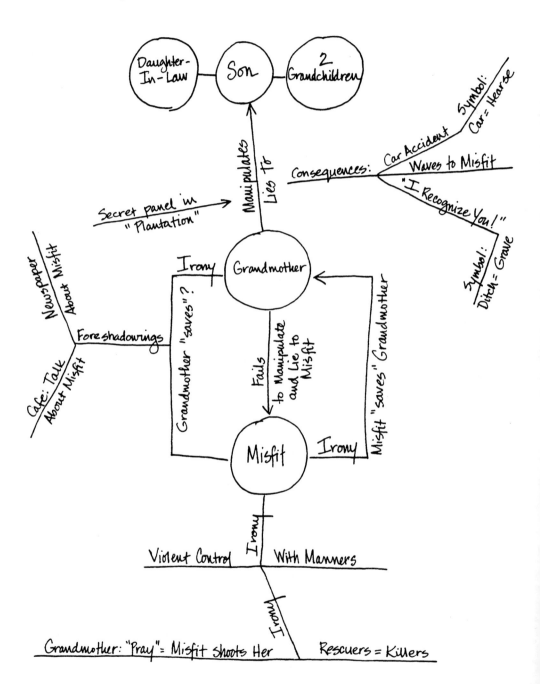

Now write the outline. Here is how the first outline might look:

IRONIC CHARACTERS (working title)

I. INTRODUCTION: THESIS STATEMENT

    A. Grandmother

        1. Manipulates everybody with manners and superficial ethics

        2. Hypocrite, lies about secret panel–ironic

    B. Misfit

        1. Violent control, with manners (ironic)

        2. Killer tells truth, searches for truth–ironic, compared with "Lady"

II. IRONIES

    A. Rescuers: Killers

    B. She says pray–pistol shot

    C. Grandmother touches Killer, he shoots, can't stand compassion, off balance. No real pleasure

    D. Foreshadowed

        1. newspaper–Misfit escapes

        2. cafe–they discuss Misfit

    E. Symbol (ironic?)

        1. car=hearse-like

        2. ditch=grave

    F. Bad consequences of Grandmothers manipulations

        1. accident

        2. waves to Misfit

        3. blurts out, I recognized you!

III. CONCLUSION

    A. Killer finally saves Grandmother

    B. Grandmother *may* save Killer (see O'Connor's essay)

F. Augment Your Outline by Reviewing Your Earlier Notes Again

By reviewing your earlier notes, you may discover one or two necessary elements for your outline. For instance, scanning your notes in the margin of the text reveals that many lines before the Misfit enters the story prove later on to be ironic.

G. Rework your Outline

Outlines seldom suffice on the first try. This is how the final outline might look. (This is a complete-sentences outline). Notice the new title, which expresses a refocussing of the main subject: irony.

IRONY AND RELIGION

I. THESIS: The two main characters' relationship is ironic

  A. The grandmother dominates the first half.

   1. She manipulates everybody with manners and old-fashioned ethics
   2. She is a hypocrite, ironically, because, for instance, she lies about the secret panel.

  B. In the second half, the emphasis is on the Misfit.

   1. He controls people, too, but with violence and, ironically, good manners.
   2. He politely tells the truth; also a deep religious truth as opposed to grandmother.

II. There is an ironic relation between violence and religion.

  A. The rescuers turn out to be the killers.
  B. The grandmother says prayers will save you, but her family is being shot in the woods.
  C. The grandmother shows compassion for the Misfit and he shoots her.

III. The killings are foreshadowed in the story.

  A. The grandmother reads about the escape from the newspaper.

B. The grandmother talks with the man in the cafe about the killers.

C. What people say earlier turns out to be ironic.

1. The grandmother sees a graveyard and they end up in a grave.
2. She cons her son by telling him the plantation will be educational for the kids; the killer educates them all with violence.
3. The son says he will stop only one time; that is only too true.
4. The grandmother hopes she's injured so her son won't get mad; the Misfit injures her fatally but her soul is saved.
5. The kids are disappointed nobody was killed in the wreck; the Misfit kills them all.

D. There are symbols in the story: the ditch is like a grave; the car is like a hearse.

E. The grandmother's manipulations have an ironic effect.

1. She makes her son turn off the highway; the car wrecks.
2. She waves at the car to save them; it's the Misfit, who kills them.
3. She tries to con the Misfit with prayers to save herself, but saves her soul instead.

IV. Conclusion:

A. The result of the grandmother's and the Misfit's actions.

1. The killer saves one of his victims, the Grandmother, by shooting her.
2. The Grandmother tries to save herself, but may have helped to save the killer's soul.

WRITE A ROUGH DRAFT

You are not alone in dreading the task of writing. Most writers dread it, some even hate it; but somewhere in the process, all writers enjoy it. Because of the dread, however, self-discipline is a trait of every writer.

As you approach the writing of your first draft, ask yourself, Do you have something worthwhile to say? If the answer is yes, get comfortable (by your own standards). If you write when you are tired, the result will be as vague as it is when you read a textbook when you're tired. Write rapidly, if you can, without stopping to deal with errors or details. Ideas will come as you write, because writing is one way to grope for an idea.

Here is a rough draft (errors and all) of an essay on irony and religion.

"Irony and Religion"

The two main characters were ironic in their relationship to each other. The grandmother dominated the firsthalf of the story by manipulating everybody with manners and ethics of the past that are superficial. Ironically, she is a hypocrite who deceives her family and even lies (about the secret panel in the plantation). The Misfit controls people, too, only with violence, but ironically, he is also polite (the way the grandmother tries to make people behave). He tells the truth, politely; compared with this "lady," he is, ironically, searching for deep religious truth to live by. He takes Jesus seriously.

There are many ironies in this story by O'Connor about the realtion between violence and religion. For instance, the rescuers of the wreck victims turned out to be killers. Just as the grandmother tells the Misfit that if he prays he will be saved, a pistol shot comes from the wood—they kill the father and son. Finally, the Grandmother sees the Misfit's spiritual agony and touches him out of compassion, but the Misfit shoots her. She, too, knocked him off balance. First, he told her "no pleasure but meanness," but her compassion takes that pleasure from him and he says at the very end, "It's no pleasure in life."

Miss O'Connor foreshadowed the massacre early in the story and several times before the accident. The grandmother tells about the escape in the paper. They talk about the Misfit in the cafe. But there were many ironies that you don't catch until after the story is over. However, because of the foreshadowing, some readers will at least subconsciously get these ironies as they go along, they become even richer in a second reading. The grandmother sees a graveyard along the highway and told about the one that went with the plantation; ironically, she doesn't find the plantation but she does find a grave—her own and her family's. She cons her son by telling him the plantation will be educational. The dirt road does not lead to the plantation but to a ditch where they are all educated in the "mysteries" of religion. [Quote O'Connor's essay]. Bailey said I will stop this one and only time and that turned out to be too true. The grandmother wished she had been injured in the wreck, so Bailey wouldn't get mad at her; the Misfit politely injures her body fatally, but helps her save her soul. The kids were disappointed nobody is killed; the Misfit does not disappoint them all.

Symbolism, too, which is used by most modern writers and is religious in this story is very important in this story. O'Connor described the killers' car as being like a hearse. The ditch is deep, like a mass grave. Perhaps the Misfit was a symbol of death. It is up to the reader.

There were ironic consequences of the grandmother's manipulation of people. She gets Bailey to turn off the highway to find the plantation and the car wrecks; if she had not waved at the Misfit's car, they would have driven past the ditch; she should not have blurted out that she "recernized" the Misfit. She tried to con the Misfit with prayer and Jesus to save herself, but it turned out to be her soul's salvation.

Irony is the reverse of what you expect. It is ironic that the rescuer kills the wreck victims, but even more ironic that the killer saved the one victim who brought all this about. It is also ironic that the grandmother tried to save her body ands ends up saving her soul. But more important to the spiritual framework

[Quote Gordon essay] of the story is that she ironically helps the killer to save himself. According to the author herself.

* * *

You may see many mistakes in grammar and mechanics; expression is vague and awkward; and there are other problems. But the writer's ability is not well-represented here because a rough first draft is an attempt to get down something one can rewrite. The writer decides to cut out the symbolism; it weakens the focus on irony. Given space limitations, several of the early ironies may be cut. Don't put quotes around your own title.

WRITE A SERIOUS FIRST DRAFT

Religion and Irony in "A Good Man Is Hard To Find"

Flannery O'Connor uses ironic reversals in the relationship between the grandmother and the Misfit to express her vision of religious mysteries in "A Good Man Is Hard To Find." In the first half, the grandmother dominates everybody by manipulating them with superficial manners and mores from a past that is "Gone With the Wind." Ironically, it is she who is a hyprocrite; she deceives her family, she even lies, luring them with the promise of a secret panel in the plantation she wants to revisit. By contrast, the Misfit controls people, but with violence; ironically, he is as polite a man as the grandmother could hope to find. Politely, he tells the truth; compared with this "lady," this killer is in search of a deep religious truth to seriously live by.

The engine of belief that makes O'Connor's religious perception operate in this story is the irony that violence can be an avenue to salvation.[1] First, the irony is merely harsh. The rescuers turn out to be killers; just as the grandmother tells the

---

[1] Flannery O'Connor, "On A Good Man Is Hard to Find," David Madden, The Fiction Tutor (Fort Worth: Holt, Rinehart and Winston, 1990), pp. 126–29.

Misfit that prayer will save him, she hears the shots that kill the mother. All ironies lend force to the central irony. At the moment when the grandmother is moved to compassion by the Misfit's religious agony and touches him compassionately, the Misfit shocked off balance, shoots her. The effect of her compassion is to take the pleasure out of his "meanness." "It's no pleasure in life," he teaches the young killer at the end.

In the first paragraph, she foreshadows the meeting of the grandmother and the Misfit. Having announced the escape reported in the newspaper, she talks about the Misfit with Red Sammy in the cafe. Once the Misfit enters the story, many lines earlier become ironic; perhaps because O'Connor heavily foreshadows the violent encounter with the Misfit, we sense subconsiously, many of those ironies. For instance, to con her son into visiting the plantation, the grandmother says, "It would very educational for the children." The dirt road leads not to a cliché plantation but to a ditch where all of them make "contact" with "reality" through violence the grandmother alone makes "contact" with they "mystery" of Christian salvation.

The grandmother hopes she is injured to delay her son's "wrath" the Misfit politely slays her body but helps her save her soul. The grandmother's hypocritical and deceitful manipulation of people finally backfires. Because she conned her son into turning off the highway to visit the plantation, the car wrecks; because she waves "dramatically" at the car, the Misfit does not fail to see them deep in the ditch; she blurts out proudly that she recognizes him, the Misfit must kill all of them. But O'Connor reverses that kind of irony when the grandmother's effort to con the Misfit with prayer and Jesus to save herself saves her soul as it condemns her body.

O'Connor leads the reader to expect these neat ironies to continue; the most powerful effect of the story is that the irony reverses the reader's expectation. It is neatly ironic that the rescuer kills the wreck victims; it is even more neat that the killer helps save the soul of the victim who lured the victims down this dirt road. It is *profoundly* ironic that when the grandmother's deceitful effort to save her life, as five members of her family are shot in the dark woods, fails and she doubts Christ raised the dead, that she then sees most clearly the Misfit's religious agony and her kinship with all men, even the Misfit. Perhaps what is even more profound in the implicit "theological framework" is the irony that the grandmother's compassionate "gesture, like the mustard-seed, will grow to a great crow-filled tree in the Misfit's heart, and will be enought of a pain to him there to turn him into the prophet he was meant to become."[2]

---

[2] Caroline Gordon, "A Good Man Is Hard to Find," David Madden, ed., The Fiction Tutor (Fort Worth: Holt, Rinehart and Winston, 1990), pp. 129–132.

* * *

This serious first draft (as opposed to the exploratory rough first draft) shows that the writer has far more ability than the rough draft demonstrates. Some grammar and mechanical problems remain, and the paper would benefit from restructuring. The material about foreshadowing and about the back-fire effect of the grandmother's manipulations (paragraphs 3 and 4) would be more effective following (in the same order paragraph 1). Also, the paragraphs are monotonously the same length. More frequent paragraphing would lend emphasis to various elements.

WHAT TO LOOK FOR IN THE REVISION PROCESS

"The best reason for putting anything down on paper," said Bernard de Voto, best known for his nonfiction, "is that one may then change it." And Sean O'Faolain, a fiction writer, said, "The art of writing is re-writing."

In looking for things that may need revision, are some things too minor to worry about? There is a story about Joseph Conrad's working habits. Every morning, his wife locked him in his study (at his request). When she let him out for lunch, she asked,

"Joseph, what did you achieve this morning?" He replied, "I put in a comma." After lunch, she locked him in again, and when she let him out for supper, she asked, "Joseph, what did you achieve this afternoon?" And Conrad replied, "I took out the comma." Ultimately, the task he was trying to achieve was "by the power of the written word to make you hear, to make you feel—it is, before all, to make you see. That—and no more, and it is everything."

Let your first draft cool awhile. Review it objectively at a later time. Poor writing is often not visible to the writer. The more you learn to recognize your mistakes, the faster you will improve your writing.

Read your essay aloud to yourself. Then read it to (or let it be read by) friends you can trust to be frank. There is a "legal" limit, however, to the amount of help friends may give, and to the help you may gather from published sources (none, unless your instructor allows consulting outside sources). Cite carefully in your paper any outside published sources, even if you only paraphrase; place double quotes around all phrases, sentences, etc, from the published material.

Most first drafts can be boiled down to about half their length.

Rewrite with your pretended reader in mind–another person like yourself. (Pretend that your instructor is only *one* of your readers.)

A checklist of suggestions to consult as you revise follows (for quick review, key terms are underlined). Not all will apply to each paper you write. Pick and choose, given the terms of your assignment. Many apply to writing papers in all your courses.

REVISION CHECKLIST

1. Use *plain words;* avoid fancy words.
2. Choose *familiar words* over unfamiliar ones.
3. Choose *English words* over foreign words.
4. Stress *nouns and verbs* over adjectives and adverbs.
5. Choose *nouns* that convey a picture and choose *active verbs*.
6. Replace long words with *short words* when you can.

7. Make *simple declarative sentences* more often than complex sentences.
8. Vary the *length* of your *sentences*.
9. The *beginnings* and the *endings of sentences* are places for emphasizing key words.
10. Use the *active* voice.
11. Make *positive statements.*
12. Most *paragraphs* should be short, but vary the lengths of your paragraphs.
13. Do not *smother* a simple point in *overly-complex language.*
14. Do not *exaggerate.*
15. Do not *announce* what you are going to say and then say it. *Say it.*
16. Do not *assume* you have said something that you have only implied to yourself in your mind?
17. Strike out *words* you don't really need. Cut superfluous sentences, even paragraphs.
18. Replace two *words* with one when you can.
19. Don't imitate; be *natural* in your *style.*
20. *Write the way you talk,* not the way you think writing is supposed to sound.
21. Avoid "I" unless your paper is informal.
22. If it is appropriate, add one *personal* or humorous moment.
23. Avoid *cute or sarcastic* phrases or statements.
24. Avoid *clichés.*
25. Avoid metaphors or similes that are too familiar.
26. Use words correctly.
27. *Clarity* is a major aim of revision.
28. *Avoid jargon,* technical phrases.
29. Revise sentences you have written mainly to *impress* the reader.
30. Make the *sequence* of your ideas effective.
31. *Restructure* your paper if necessary.
32. Consider writing a *new outline* to show restructuring.
33. When writing about narrative events, *use present tense.*
34. Make certain your *pronoun references* are clear.
35. Avoid *dangling modifiers.*
36. Do not use *sentence fragments.*

37. Do not overuse *conjunctions*.
38. *Titles* of books are *underlined;* titles of short stories are enclosed in quotation marks.
39. The *title* of your paper is not enclosed in quotation marks.
40. *Quotations within quotations* are indicated with single quotation marks. *Proof read!* Most errors result from failure to proof-read. To spot detail and mechanical errors, proof-read one time by starting with the last sentence and read to the first.
41. Give you paper a *title* that is both informative and expressive, not just a label.
42. *Type* your paper on 8-1/2 by 11 white, bond (not erasable) paper, double space, with 1-1/2 inch margin on left, one inch margin on the right, 27 or 28 lines of type to a page. If you must *write* it by hand, use black ink, leaving a space between each line.

For excellent advice, see William Strunk's *Elements of Style,* George Orwell's "Politics and the English Language", in *Shooting an Elephant and Other Essays,* and Robert Gunning's *The Technique of Clear Writing.*

REVISE YOUR PAPER

Here is the revised version of the essay (a few errors remain).

Violence, A Dirt Road

to Salvation in Flannery O'Connor's

"A Good Man Is Hard To Find"

To express her vision of religious mysteries in "A Good Man Is Hard To Find," Flannery O'Connor creates ironic reversals in the relationship between the Grandmother and the Misfit.

In the first half, the grandmother manipulates everybody with superficial manners and mores from a past that is "Gone With the Wind." But she proves to be a hyprocrite, deceiving her family, even lying when she lures them with the promise of a secret panel, into looking for a plantation she wants to revisit.

The Misfit controls people, too, but with violence. Ironically, he is also as polite a man as the grandmother could ever hope to meet. Politely, he tells the truth in response to her deceptiveness; compared with this "lady," this killer searches for a deep religious truth to live by.

Afraid the reader might be distracted by suspense, O'Connor heavily foreshadows the meeting of the grandmother and the Misfit. Having announced the escape reported in the newspaper, in the first paragraph, she talks about the Misfit with Red Sammny in the Tower Cafe.

Once the Misfit discovers the family, the reader realizes that many earlier lines are ironic; the foreshadowing makes us somewhat aware of the ironies as we read. Such examples as: "It would be very educational," for the children, the grandmother tells her son to con him into visiting the plantaion. The dirt road leads not to a stereotyped platation but to a ditch where all of them make "contact" with "reailty" through violence and the grandmother alone makes contact with the "mystery" of Christian salvation. Ironically, the grandmother hopes she is injured to defuse her son's "wrath"; more ironically, the Misfit politely slays her body, but helps her save her soul.

The grandmother's hypocritical and deceitful manipulation of people finally backfires, with bitter irony. Because she conned her son into turning off the highway to visit the plantation, the car wrecks; becasue she waves "dramatically" at the car, the Misfit does not fail to see them deep in the ditch; because she blurts out proudly that she recognizes him, the Misfit must kill all of them. But O'Connor reverses the kind of irony when the grandmother's effort to con the Misfit with Jesus to save herself saves her soul even as it condemns her body.

The "engine" of belief that makes O'Connor's religious "perception operate" in this story is the irony that violence can be a dirt road to salvation.[1]

O'Connor seems to want the reader to expect the simple ironies to continue; the most crucial irony is all the more powerful because it reverses even the reader's expectations. It is neatly ironic that the rescuer kills the wreck victims; it is even neater that the killer helps save the soul of the woman he kills. When the grandmother's desperate effort, as she hears the shots come from the "dark open mouth" of the woods, to save her life fails; when she says "Maybe He didn't raise the dead," she sees the religious agony in the Misfit's face. It is profoundly ironic that it is at that moment that she feels a compassionate "kinship" which makes even the Misfit one of her "own children."

Perhaps it is even more profoundly ironic, within O'Connor's implicit "theological framework," that the grandmother's compassionate "gesture, like the mustard-seed, will grow to a great crow-filled tree in the Misfit's heart, and will be enough of a pain to him there to turn him into the prophet he was meant to become."[2] That, unlikely though it may seem to some readers, is how Flannery O'Connor prefers to think.

---

[1] Flannery O'Connor, "On 'A Good Man Is Hard to Find,'" in David Madden, editor, The Fiction Tutor (Fort Worth: Holt, Rinehart and Winston, 1990), pp. 126–29.

[2] Caroline Gordon and Allen Tate, "Comment on O'Connor's 'A Good Man Is Hard to Find,'" in David Madden, editor, The Fiction Tutor (Fort Worth: Holt, Rinehart and Winston, 1990), pp. 129–132.

* * *

What grade does this paper deserve and why?

Observe that in the entire process, the writer has selected and focussed the subject of irony, that the outlines grew in usefulness, that the rough draft captured most of the wording, that the serious first draft demonstrated an ability to concentrate on ideas and expression. The final draft has a few minor mechanical problems—demonstrating the importance of proof reading before you submit a paper—but the reorganization has produced a more forceful structure, the paragraphing is variable in length and emphasizes separate ideas, the choice of words is more distinctive, and new phrasing has sharpened ideas. The final paper has gone further toward demonstrating not only the thesis as stated but a richer explanation of the ironic relationship between the grandmother and the Misfit. The writer expresses an insight at the end that goes beyond the relationship itself, leaving the reader with something sufficiently new to think about.

3

MASTER LIST OF WRITING TOPICS
THAT APPLY TO MOST FICTION

Papers may deal with the elements of fiction (characters, conflict, plot, theme) or with technical devices (point of view, style, symbolism, etc.) or with a combination of two or more of these. The following list of writing topics applies to most fiction:

1. The development of *character* through the writer's handling of conflict (or of plot, style, point of view).
2. How *point of view* determines the writer's *style* in this particular story (as opposed to his or her general use of style, if you are familiar with it).
3. How the author illuminates character through *dialogue* (or uses dialogue to convey other elements in the story, such as exposition or thematic concerns).
4. The devices the author uses to *imply* what is not literally stated (symbols, irony, contrast, allusion, motifs, etc.).
5. How the writer develops the overall *context* of the story (death, anxiety, marriage, etc.). Give specific examples.
6. The function in the story of *allusions* (or of a pattern of symbols, motifs, or ironies).
7. The relation between a technique and the *theme* of the story.

4
CONSIDERATIONS AS YOU WRITE

As a review list, here are some things to consider. Your purpose in writing a paper is to lead a reader like yourself to respond more fully to a single aspect of a story.

1. *Survey* the possibilities. (The list of "considerations for reading" may get you started.)
2. *Choose* a topic. (Point of view, for instance.)
3. *Narrow* the topic. (Point of view and style, for instance.)
4. *Support* general statements with specifics.

    a.   *cite* passages (give a general description, provide page number and paragraph–p. 5, third paragraph, for instance).

    b.   *quote* passages (give page number).

    c.   *allude* to passages (that you have already cited or quoted or that you expect most readers will remember).

5. If you are writing about *theme,* describe how the writer uses a technique (point of view, style, suspense) to express that theme.
6. If you are writing about *characters,* describe how point of view and style express facets of character (a first-person narrative may be full of lies and deceptive phrases, for instance).
7. Writing about *conflict* involves, of course, writing about the characters involved in that conflict; enhance your points with descriptions of technical devices that enhance the way the writer develops conflict—use of suspense, pace, transitions, etc.

GLOSSARY OF LITERARY TERMS

ALLUSION—An allusion is a reference to a person, event, or aspect of culture that writers assume most of their readers will recognize. A literary allusion may evoke a familiar line from a poem, or a character from a novel or play. Allusions provide an added dimension to a story.

AMBIGUITY—Ambiguity occurs in a story when an element (statement, action, or symbol, for instance) lends itself to more than one interpretation. Controlled, deliberate ambiguity enables the reader to explore possibilities and experience the tensions among them, causing a deeper involvement in the story. Unintentional ambiguity results in obscurity. Unintentional ambiguity is often the result of confusion in the author's mind as to the meaning of his or her ideas or the author's inability to express those ideas clearly.

ANTICIPATION—As writers bring the development of one episode to an end, they may introduce an element that anticipates an episode to come. Writers may satisfy that anticipation immediately or may deliberately frustrate it for an even more interesting effect. The reader then expects that a certain event or development will occur. Indications or suggestions of what is to come are often called "foreshadowings" or "plants."

ASSUMPTIONS—Unconsciously, though sometimes consciously, writers make assumptions about their readers' knowledge, attitudes, and perceptiveness. Working out of those assumptions, they try to appeal to the attitudes and knowledge they think their readers have about love, violence, morality, politics, and so on, in a style which readers will find acceptable. Writers can often be mistaken in their assumptions, however.

ATMOSPHERE—Atmosphere is the mood or climate of a story. Sometimes writers feel that mood or atmosphere is enough to sustain a story, but atmosphere is more meaningful when combined with characters who have problems. Authors establish atmosphere by the objects they select to describe, by how they describe them, and by the SETTING in which they place them.

CHARACTERIZATION—Characterization is the creation of imaginary people through descriptions of physical appearance, actions, speech, thoughts, or what other characters say or think about them.

CLICHÉ—A cliché is an expression that once had originality and freshness but has become trite and stale through overuse. Some writers (and some readers) do not object as strongly as others to clichés, but most writers try to be as original as they can without calling too much attention to their style. Some writers deliberately use cliches to give an aura of everyday reality to the world they are creating. Other writers prepare a special context for a cliché that resurrects its original vitality.

CLIMAX—The climax of a story comes at that point when the complications of the PLOT are most fully developed and a resolution of the problem is in sight. Each episode or scene may have its own climax. When a story depends heavily upon suspense for its effects, the climax is especially intense. Some stories reach a quiet, subtle, almost submerged climax.

CONFLICT—A conflict is a struggle between opposing forces. A character may have an external conflict with another character, a group, or with nature or society in general, or may have an internal conflict between opposing feelings or attitudes. Conflict is sometimes considered to be only the struggle between the hero (protagonist) and the villain (antagonist), but the main character is often his or her own antagonist. A story usually contains minor conflicts, also. Conflict, TENSION, and suspense are sometimes thought to be the same; they are not, but they do enhance each other. See TENSION, PLOT.

CONTEXT and IMPLICATION—Page by page, writers create contexts that generate implications. To avoid being too literal, writers may draw on general and immediate contexts to create an implication–about one of their characters, for instance. To respond to implications, the reader must be actively involved in the story.

CONTRAST and COMPAR_SON—The device of contrast or comparison enables the reader to achieve a clearer picture of character, setting, and other elements.

DRAMATIC MONOLOGUE—A character talks, throughout most or all of the story, to a listener (or listeners) the presence of whom is somehow stated or implied. A dramatic duologue consists of *only* two characters talking to each other.

FIGURATIVE LANGUAGE—Figurative language is language expanded beyond its usual literal meaning to achieve intensity and vividness. A figurative expression usually contains a stated or implied comparison to express a relationship between things essentially unlike. Metaphors and similes are two common types of figures of speech. The metaphor "John is a lion" is an implied comparison that is more immediate and dramatic than "John has some of the characteristics of a lion." "John is like a lion" is a simile, a stated comparison. The word "like" specifies that a similarity exists between John and a lion. "As if" and "as though" are other signals that a simile is being introduced in a sentence.

Writers of fiction use similes more often than metaphors because metaphors tend to try a reader's patience. "John is a lion" may make some readers reply, "No, he isn't." A reader is more likely to accept the simile "John is like a lion." Metaphors and similes are most effective when the reader feels that they are appropriate to the context of the story, that they seem to be part of a pattern.

FORESHADOWING—See ANTICIPATION.

GENRE—Types of fiction: satire, science fiction, western, crime, occult, allegory, etc.

IMAGERY—Imagery is the collection of descriptive details in a literary work that appeal to the senses. An author uses an image to arouse emotion in the reader and to establish mood.

INEVITABILITY—When we feel that what happens in a story, especially in the end, must happen because of the way the elements have been set in motion, we feel a sense of inevitability.

INTERIOR MONOLOGUE—A character talks, somewhat consciously, to himself at some length in a story — or throughout.

IRONY—Irony exists when there is a discrepancy between the appearance and the reality of a situation or when the reverse or opposite of what a reader expects happens. Verbal irony occurs when writers deliberately say the opposite of what they mean. Often, a reader sees the irony in a situation while the characters do not. Most stories use some form of irony, crude or subtle.

JUXTAPOSITION—A special effect can be created when two elements are set side by side, or juxtaposed. Some juxtapositions are accidental, others are deliberate. Sometimes a writer may justapose two images that have no special impact separately but that spark an idea or an emotion when set side by side. The two words, images, or events may be so deliberately and carefully chosen that they spark a third element that exists only in the reader's mind.

In the movies this technique is called "montage." The Russian director Eisenstein describes montage in this way: "Two pieces of film of any kind, placed together, inevitably combine into a new concept, a new quality, arising out of that juxtaposition." Juxtaposition or montage is a technigue that involves the reader as a collaborator in the creative process.

METAPHOR—See FIGURATIVE LANGUAGE.

MOTIF—A motif is an element that is repeated, usually with variation, throughout a story. A motif may be a recurring subject, idea, or theme. Motifs help to set up the reader's anticipation and provide the writer with a means of emphasis and focus. Some writers consciously employ motifs: others leave such enhancements entirely to chance. Motifs should not be confused with symbols, although symbols may be part of a pattern of motifs. See SYMBOLISM.

NONCONVENTIONAL FICTION—Avant garde, experimental fiction that does not fit conventional types or meet the usual reader expectations.

PACE—Pace is the rate of movement of all the parts of a story. (Some parts of a story may move at a different rate than others.) An author may accelerate pace by using abrupt transitions or short bits of dialogue: the pace may be slowed by using narrative description. The author's regulation of pace affects the reader's responses to all the other elements in a story. Pace may contribute to the sense of inevitability we feel about the way the story turns out; pace may excite psychological tension and sustain narrative tension.

PARALLELS—A parallel is an element that moves alongside another element: they mutually enhance each other's effect, sometimes through contrast or comparison. A parallel is something like a motif in a pattern; it is sometimes mistaken for a symbol.

PLOT—Plot is the arrangement of narrative events to demonstrate the development of an action involving characters. A description of the plot sometimes traces the development of the story's meaning simultaneously with its storyline, for plot is an action that illustrates a basic idea. It is the simultaneous ordering of all the elements, not just characters in action, in such a way as to produce a unified effect. See STORY.

POINT OF VIEW—Every story is told from a certain point of view, usually only one. There are three major types of point of view. 1. *Omniscient*: the author sees, hears, feels, and knows all. He or she moves anywhere in time and space and gives the reader objective views of characters' actions or subjective views of their thoughts. 2. *First person*: the author surrenders partial control over the elements of a story by having one of the characters tell it. We experience only what that character sees, hears, feels, and knows while the author works in the background. The character-narrator combines his or her own subjective thought with his or her role as storyteller. 3. *Third person-central intelligence*: This technique allows the reader to experience everything from inside a single character (the central intelligence), but the story is told in the third person. All the elements are filtered through a single person, revealing that person's personality.

Because it most directly affects the choice and use of all other elements, point of view is the most important technique. Each type of point of view allows the writer particular freedoms and imposes particular limitations. Readers must feel that the point of view through which the story reaches them is the inevitable one.

RAW MATERIAL—Raw material is the subject matter the writer processes through imagination, conception, and TECHNIQUE into a story. Real people at a certain time and place provide a writer with raw material. "By raw material," says Wright Morris, "I mean that comparatively crude ore that has not yet been processed by the imagination— what we refer to as life, ore as experience, in contrast to art. By technique I mean the way the artist smelts this material down for human consumption . . . . Technique and raw material are dramatized at the moment that the shaping imagination is aware of itself."

REPETITION—Repetition is a device that intensifies readers' responses by enabling them to remember important elements as the story moves ahead. An element is introduced, then repeated, with variations in a pattern, throughout the story. Repetition is a major unifying device.

REVERSAL—Reversal is a device that causes delight or enlightenment. When readers are led to expect or anticipate a certain development and the reverse occurs, the surprise may delight them; if the reversal is contrived or forced, they may be resentful. A reversal may also deepen the readers' understanding of what they have experienced so far.

SATIRE—Satire is the use of irony, wit, humor, or ridicule to expose human folly. Implicit in a true satirical story is a vision of life that is superior to the target.

SENTIMENTALITY—Everyone is sentimental about something, but sentimentality is a tendency to be influenced excessively by thoughts and feelings rather than reason. Some authors deliberately play upon a reader's inclinations toward sentimentality; others deliberately avoid it and often treat it ironically or satirically. When our reason tells us that the cause of a character's feelings is trivial and the response excessive, we may conclude that he or she is being too sentimental.

SETTING—The setting of a story is the time and place in which the events occur. The time may mean the period (past, present, future) or the season or time of day in which a story is set. The place may be geographic (in a house, on a plane, in a city) or psychological (in a character's mind). An author may make time or place indeterminable, however. ATMOSPHERE is often conveyed in descriptions of setting; one author sees setting as "metaphoric expression of characters."

SIMILE—See FIGURATIVE LANGUAGE.

SIMULTANEITY—When all the elements in a story are coordinated and controlled by techniques, the effect is a sense of simultaneity: a feeling at any given moment that all the elements interact in our minds and emotions; the reader holds all the elements in the consciousness at once. If readers have this sense of simultaneity throughout the story, they feel at the end a sense of inevitability: everything has happened as it has because it has to. See INEVITABILITY.

STEREOTYPE—A stereotype is a character or situation that has been overused in fiction. The stereotype is cut to a pattern or conforms to a formula that seldom varies. The shootout between the sheriff and the outlaw in front of a Western saloon is a stereotypical situation involving stereotyped characters. A stereotypical character is like a CLICHÉ.

STREAM OF CONSCIOUSNESS—Thoughts and images flowing through a character's mind, with little or no author comment or narrative.

STORY—Story may be distinguished from PLOT. Story is, simply, the order of narrative events in which characters work out conflicts. See PLOT.

STYLE—Style is an author's choice of words (diction), arrangement of words in a sentence (syntax), and the handling of sentences and paragraph units to achieve a specific effect. Style and choice of POINT OF VIEW are major aspects of TECHNIQUE. (The style of a story is somewhat determined by the point of view an author decides to employ.) One aspect of style is the use of rhetorical devices (proven ways of stimulating the desired emotion, attitude, or idea in the reader) and figurative language (the use of metaphors and similes, for instance.)

SYMBOLISM—Symbolism is the use of an object, image, event, or character to represent or suggest another. The use of symbolism enables a writer to show relationships among people, nature, society, the intellect, and the spirit. Symbols may be incidental, or a story may be unified by a symbolic design. Symbols help to focus ideas and feelings so that the story's impact is stronger and deeper. Writers and readers have passed through several decades of overuse of symbols. The habit of symbol hunting in literary study, aided of course by overinfatuation with symbols on the part of writers, has led to an antisymbol attitude among readers. "Who can't make up symbols?" asks James M. Cain. And some students may ask, "And who wants to hunt them down once writers do make them up?" This attitude ignores the vital importance of symbols and symbolic patterns when they are used effectively. The term "symbolism" is often used for elements that aren't really symbolic, or that might better be called by other names. See MOTIF and PARALLELS.

TASTE—Taste is a personal preference or liking for something, often influenced by mysterious emotional factors. Tastes and critical judgments may clash. For instance, readers may have a taste for a certain type of fiction that their critical faculties tell them is inferior. Of all the forces outside a story that affect a reader's response, taste is the most powerful. Taste is a murky area, but a deeper understanding of the process that shapes taste may illuminate a great deal about the creative process itself. It is likely that as readers reach a better understanding of the nature of taste and of fiction their tastes will change.

TECHNIQUE—A technique is any method a writer uses, consciously or unconsciously, to stimulate a response in his reader. "When we speak of technique," says novelist and critic Mark Schorer, "we speak of nearly everything. For technique . . . is the only means the writer has of discovering, exploring, developing his subject, of conveying its meaning, and, finally, of evaluating it." Technique enables writers to discover possibilities in their raw material that would otherwise remain submerged in it. It's impossible to write a story without using technique, but some writers create mainly out of inspiration and a kind of subjective preoccupation while others are more aware and in control of what they're doing through conscious use of techniques. Style differs somewhat from technique in that style, the arrangement of words for specific effects, is the medium through which techniques are employed. Style is one aspect of the larger realm of technique.

TENSION—When two or more elements pull the reader simultaneously in different directions, the reader feels a tension that sustains emotional involvement in the story. The author may set up a tension between literal and metaphorical meaning, between characters, or between techniques themselves.

THEME—The theme is a story's main idea, or its underlying meaning. Sometimes theme is used to mean "subject matter," but not in this book. Characters and events express theme, but TECHNIQUE and STYLE may also be expressive of theme. Theme, like SYMBOLISM, is sometimes overstressed in the study of fiction. Eventually, discussion of any element of fiction reveals some aspect of theme, but a preoccupation with theme will reveal very little about the *nature* of fiction.

TONE—A writer's attitude toward RAW MATERIAL or subject is revealed in tone. The pervasive tone of a work can be tragic, comic, ironic, skeptical, pessimistic, compassionate, sentimental, and so on. The author's distance in relation to the story affects tone. It is important that the tone be appropriate to the kind of experience a writer is trying to create.

TRANSITION—A transition is movement in a story from one time, place, position, or idea to another. A transitional device is any method a writer uses to accomplish a transition. "One summer afternoon . . . " and "On my way uptown today.. . . . " are two ways of signaling transitions in time and place. Transitions are often difficult to make because the writer must reorient the reader. In some instances a subtle transition is most effective; in others, an abrupt change may work best.

NOTES